Praises in the Storm

A COLLECTION OF POEM

Mihaela S. Hegstrom

TRANSLATED BY MIHAELA S. HEGSTROM   REVISED BY DAVID W. HEGSTROM

LitFire
PUBLISHING

LitFire LLC
1-800-511-9787
www.litfirepublishing.com
order@litfirepublishing.com

Contents

APPRECIATION FOR <u>PRAISES IN THE STORM</u>

As the deer pants for streams of water, so my soul pants for You, O God. My soul thirsts for God, for the living God. When can I go and meet with God?"

Psalm 42:1-2

It is through the valleys and storms of life that the human soul looks for a door to exit the prison of unspoken pain. Quite often, on the narrow path of earthly sorrows, when words have been lost in its dark corridors, the human soul rests when it finds its expression in another traveler's words, even one unknown. Then, the soul's "groans that words cannot express" take the form of the victorious song given to another wounded soldier who passed on that way before, and the soul is recharged with renewed energy. Strengthened by the hope, faith, and awareness of the constant presence of the unseen living and loving God, courage is mounted up to stand firm, along with determination to conquer any storm, any battle, any giant on the Christian's earthly journey, being armed with the divine power given to each believer in spite of human limitation.

In simple words drawn from everyday living experiences, <u>Praises in the Storm</u> does just that: it is an oasis for the soul to regain its strength through the words of each poem of profound and refreshing Biblical truth. It is only when we realize our total dependency on our Maker and acknowledge His active participation as revealed in His Word that we are equipped with invincible powers from above to defeat destructive fears, discouragement, unbelief, disappointments, self-reliance, pride, oppression, selfishness, and deceptions of any form or shape and to leave the battleground triumphantly, with a song of praise for those who will come behind us and gratitude for having been enabled to win the spiritual battles of life. Like with David's songs of recollection – the Psalms –the reader will return many times to Praises in the Storm to identify with its poetic expression when his own words are not enough. Read it and pass it on to lift up the mind and soul and reestablish perspective.

> *"Why are you downcast, O my soul? Why so disturbed within me? Put your hope in God, for I will yet praise Him, my Savior and my God. ... In God, Whose word I praise, in the Lord, Whose Word I praise– in God I trust; I will not be afraid."*
>
> Psalm 42:5, 56:10-11

Georgetta Livingstone, Ph.D.

Being part of the Romanian diaspora for thirty years, Mihaela S. Hegstrom has demonstrated enviable perseverance by completing this project. We see the author to be someone with a sensitive soul, who chose to express in a poetic form some of the most profound personal and family experiences. The verses have rich spiritual content, based upon the revelation of the Holy Scriptures and addressing themes such as salvation through faith in Jesus Christ, reconciliation with God, the experience of worship, and living the Christian life. Two important characteristics may be observed in Mihaela Hegstrom's poems: constant dialogue with the Divinity through questions, prayers, inner searches, and confessions and steadfast belief in God in the midst of the trials of life.

Adrian and Adina Stănculescu

Each time that I meditate on these poems, I feel that they are a blessed channel through which God Himself pours encouragement, strength, peace, and determination to serve Him more with all love.

Marcela Hosu

DEDICATION

I dedicate these poems to my children Mary and David, who along with God, have brought so much joy to my life, beautifying and enriching it. The two of them are the shining stars of my life. Through their presence they have also brought to me a sense of deep responsibility like nothing or no one else has before.

Mary and David,

With God's help I have taught you His wonderful Word, and the Holy Spirit planted in your souls this blessed seed, which sprung up at the right time. For this I am thankful both to God and to you.

May the Almighty keep you and preserve you to the end, that together we will be able to see Him in His heavenly glory.

In His love,

Your Mother

FOREWORD

PRAISES IN THE STORM

Life is not just a harmony or a perfect melody.
Life is a school; it is trials, experiences, and fights
In which often pain and joy mingle together
When the soul sings, the mind dreams, and the waves hit.

Prof. Dumitru Buhai

In front of me, on the computer's electronic pages, I have eighty-two poems, written by Mihaela Hegstrom. I enter into the charm of words carefully arranged into lines which transmit ideas, groan and sing, give hope, and direct towards faith in God in a book of poems in which the sacred is a manifestation of faith and love for God and fellow man.

The poems are written with a language which is the color of the author's soul and a cord that ties us to eternity. The combining of the words in such a personal manner creates a sense of lyrical pathos and inner reflection, as well as repulsion in the face of injustice. The model followed by the poet is that of popular poetry. Here is a stanza from the poem entitled "I Came to You" in which the natural and the spiritual directly confront each other, giving the poet the opportunity to rise upon the wings of divine love beyond the ugliness of hatred and deceit to the level of "praises in the storm:"

"Around me is only hatred,
Confusion, quarrels, lies;
But You put in my mouth words that form
Praises in the storm."

In the poem entitled "From Childhood," the lyrical pathos, tenderness, and care in the advice given to her sister for a blessed future were evident:

"...And sometimes on the road of your life,
May you proceed as in the years of your youth:

"With enthusiasm and with faith,
In a life of victory.
And when troubles appear,
Do not forget His grace!"

The theme of spirituality occupies a special place in the poetry of this volume. It is sufficient to give a single example, such as the following stanza from the poem entitled "The Thought About Eternity:"

"Our souls become precious
When they have Christ in them;
The pain, the fear, the difficulty will cease,
And the torment and dread we will forget."

The stylistic language and the arrangement of the words into rhythmic lines give us a feeling of calmness, hope, faith, and assurance as well as an entrance into an oasis of blessing.

The purpose of a poem is to present beauty in the form of the insightful expression of an idea and to spiritually enrich the reader. Religious poetry in particular, using words like wonderful seeds of divine origin, has the purpose of leading the reader to a rebirth of faith and to saving hope as well as bringing spiritual harmony and joy.

I earnestly recommend this debut book written by the poet Mihaela Hegstrom to readers young and old, considering that they will find fitting words and music for the soul in moments of tranquility and also encouragement on the narrow path of life on this earth.

Prof. Dumitru Buhai

Chicago
November 7, 2009

PREFACE

This collection of poems is the English version of the book I wrote in the Romanian language entitled <u>Laude în Furtună</u>, which was published in Romania in December of 2009. Many of these Romanian poems are also posted on two U.S. websites as well as one foreign website. I have been blessed to receive many positive comments regarding my poems, including the appreciation provided in this book. This English version contains the eighty-two poems comprising the original version followed by fifteen more poems which I wrote directly in the English language. This is a revised, improved, new edition. The first edition was published in 2010, by a different publisher. Ain this edition I made improvements in text, so, that this collection will be reader friendly, easier to read and to understand.

As much as I could I tried to create some rhymes to this translation, to create the beautiful musicality that goes so well with good poetry. This is true especially in the first part of the book. But there are poems that do not follow a certain pattern of rhyming because the translation did not allowed that, thus creating different kinds of poems of different types.

I decided to do this translation because many of my family members and friends can only speak English. I did so while struggling to establish myself as a writer against long odds, pursuing the dream of this translation which I wasn't certain could become reality. I did it in the awareness that each of us has a personal calling in life. I consider personal calling to be the God-given talent that God chose to give us which fills us with passion, a burning desire, and enthusiasm which cannot be denied or suppressed. In the process of making this dream become reality, however, I had to overcome certain fears. The first was the notion that dreams cannot become realities, which had been ingrained in me since my childhood. This would kill my aspirations, leaving me only with the guilt of entertaining the fantasy of those thoughts. My passion to write these poems and translate them into English remained deeply planted within me, although this fear hid it almost entirely.

Another fear I faced was the fear that I would expend too much time in pursuing my dream – that I would be forced to sacrifice interaction with important people in my life as well as other important things that required my attention. A third fear that I had to confront was the fear of inadequacy – the fear of defeat. English being my second language, I doubted my ability to complete this translation well enough so that it could be clearly understood by anyone who reads it. The last fear that I faced was the uncertainty of what might happen if I did actually realize my dream, considering the multitude of possible reactions and consequences that could result from this. However, I was ultimately reminded that "God has not given us a spirit of fear, but of power." This truth, along with my awareness of the fact that God invested in me this gift for the purpose of glorifying Him and bringing forth fruit as well as the admonition that the apostle Paul gives to Timothy to "stir up the gift of God which is in you," persuaded me to carry on and pursue this call. At this point I realized that "I can do all things through Christ Who strengthens me," just as His Word says. With this frame of mind I was ready to start this translation.

I created this translation with three objectives in mind. The first was to maintain the original meaning from the Romanian version as much as possible. The second was to fashion the poems in such a way as to allow their ideas to flow smoothly. My final objective was to incorporate rhyming where it was possible to do so without altering the original meaning too much. This translation was carefully reviewed by my son David, whose primary language is English. I am very appreciative of his willingness to help me, as he spent many hours whenever he could to make corrections and improvements in order to put these poems into a more understandable and easy-to-read form. Without his help, this book would not be in existence. I wish God's rich blessings upon him.

It is my pleasure and privilege to be able to share with you, the reader, what the Lord has put upon my heart to write. For a long time I had wanted to put the thoughts and meditations of my heart directed towards God onto paper, but I did not do it. For every decision there is a reason, and such was the case in my decisions both to write and to translate these poems. The Lord used different situations and means to make me understand that putting these God-inspired poems into a book is what I had to do at this point in my life. I consider poetry to be an organized, literary form of expressing ideas, emotions, and feelings in a similar way that mathematics is designed to help us to receive, convey, and logically work with information in an orderly fashion. I also realize that not everyone can write meaningful poems having essence and the ability to transmit spiritual truths of eternal value unless the gift and the necessary inspiration to do so were given to him or her. Because these poems, which God put into my soul, were originally written in Romanian, and because I now live in a foreign society with a language entirely different than my native language and my children were born in this society, I thought that few would ever understand the value of my poems and that my children would only be able to do so in part. Thus I then decided to create this translation.

It is my great desire that these poems will glorify God for who He is and that His Son Jesus Christ will be revealed through them by the power of the Holy Spirit. I truly hope that by reading these poems, you will be blessed with God's presence in and around you.

These poems reflect personal experiences with our triune God as well as revelations which God saw fit to show me. It is not on account of my merit that He chose to give me these thoughts, these ideas, these lines; it is on account of His grace alone, for which I am very thankful. I asked Him to do His work in my life in any way that He desired since I wish to be a useful vessel in His kingdom, and thus I let myself be open to His guidance.

I had my start in writing poetry when I was in high school, but at that time my poems were of different content and a different nature. After my graduation from high school, I was admitted into college, where I studied mechanical engineering and pedagogy. After I graduated with my degree in mechanical engineering, I started to use the art of writing again, opening up my heart and describing my thoughts using the rhyme and beauty of poetry.

About three years after finishing college, my family and I immigrated to the United States. Here, life presented its own difficulties and challenges, and for a long time I did not have the strength or determination to write anymore. Now, after many years, I again decided to write. This decision came from a passion far greater than I can explain in my weak words. It came from a power within, which I could not hold back anymore. Today I know that it was the will of God, the Creator, Whose love I do not deserve and Whom I serve with humility according to the measure of faith given to me, such a weak vessel. I thank Him that "God has chosen the weak things of the world to put to shame the things which are mighty," just as is said in His precious word, the Bible.

These poems also come as a fulfillment of the promise that I would tell others about what the Lord did in my life which I made to Him after He healed me of a very serious, life-threatening illness and supported me in difficult situations which He allowed me to go through, in order to build up my character and show me more and more my desperate need for Him. Through all these things He helped me bring to Him praises in the storm.

The purpose of this collection of poems is to glorify both the name of God and God's love, which was shown through the coming to earth of His Son, Jesus Christ, culminating in Christ's supreme sacrifice upon the cross and the triumph of His resurrection. I also desire that many souls will be blessed by reading them, thus coming closer to the Savior of all those who with pure and sincere faith seek Him in humility and repentance. In reading these poems, may the reader find peace in the midst of trouble, joy when there is sadness, beauty when ugliness is all around, true hope in the midst of hopelessness, courage when facing fear, and also the admonition to bring praises in the storm of life because of the care and faithfulness that the Lord shows to each of us on our journeys.

Mihaela S. Hegstrom

ACKNOWLEDGEMENTS

I would like to thank all who recognized a God-given talent in me and who did not cease to persuade me to put my thoughts, feelings, and emotions onto paper.

I would especially like to thank my children for the encouragement that they gave me while working on this book and for the time they took from their busy schedules (their studies) to read my poems or to listen while the poems were read to them; their comments were of great value to me, and I was very glad to receive them. I would like to thank my daughter for her wise remarks and for the encouragement that she gave me, as well as for her financial help, without which this book could not be published. I would like to thank David, my son, who though being very busy with his studies, took many hours to help me with the editing of this book, also spending much time reviewing the translation of the first eighty-two poems since English is his primary language. Without his input in rearranging each poem into a form that could be more easily read, this book would not be in existence.

I would also like to thank my husband, who found me many times in front of the computer spending many hours in order to bring this project to its intended end, a situation that he accepted.

May the Lord be glorified through these poems and may those who read them be blessed.

Mihaela S. Hegstrom

The Thought about Eternity

The days go by in a row one by one,
And thus go weeks and months.
In this way our lives go by continuously,
Carrying with them lots of wonders, miraculously.

The days pass, going always into eternity,
And we pass with them together.
Leaving behind a forgotten world
Of many feelings and thoughts.

With each day that goes by,
All the more towards eternity
We approach it with our nothingness
And with our poor souls in brokenness.

Yes, little by little we approach the infinite
Which should make us think
Of our souls and their purity
Going fast towards eternity

Our souls become precious
When they have Christ in them;
The pain, the fear, the difficulty will cease,
And we will know His blessed peace.

Then His joy and His hope will reign
In our mortal and fragile lives,
And we will gladly go to work,
To be of help to someone, easing up his yoke.

Then the meaning of life we will understand,
As well as our purpose on the earth:
To walk on the path that goes
Upward towards the holy heaven.

January 1982

From Childhood

From childhood I studied you
And looking at you I found out
That you had strength and will
Along with potential and belief

From childhood I realize and I knew
That you would reach great heights
Because always you looked to Jesus.

I saw how you lived and who you were –
All full of confidence and faith
With your heart aspiring upwards
And with your eyes focused on Jesus' words.

I saw how you grew, how you flourished and struggled
On the rough path of this difficult life,
And I saw how you behaved and carried
The heavy yoke of youth by trials accompanied

Now that you are done and finished
School with its responsibilities and struggle,
With dignity and humility you found
That the life waiting for you has a different sound.

After such a hard task along with such hard labor
And putting such a sustained effort
You arrived where your heart desired,
And where your mind keenly aspired.

Now, however, do not allow yourself to forget
That all you have, God gave to you,
Remember those who cultivated in you
The desire to fight, to excel and to pursue.

May many congratulations and joy
Be imparted to you on your path,
And always on the road of your life,
May you proceed with grace and might.

With enthusiasm and with faith,
In a life full joys and victory.
And when troubles appear,
Do not forget His grace is near.

August 21, 1993

I CAME TO YOU

From the path of confusion and sin
You, Jesus, searched for me and found me,
You took me from where I have been
And gave me, Your love and made me free.

I searched for You in many places,
Through educated writings and minds,
Through music, song and thru many guesses
And I found You in Your Word that binds.

Through it, You showed me
That You gave me forgiveness
When I ran to You, with You to be
With my troubled soul, desiring Your richness.

You promised me peace, hope, abundant life and rest,
Love, understanding, compassion and light.
In You I found the way, the truth, and the life, all the best
Which dissipated my fog and gave me a different sight.

Around me is only animosity and hatred,
Confusion, quarrels, envy, deceit and lies;
But You put in my mouth words that form
Praises in the storm that in its furry my faith tries.

In the depths of my soul and of my heart
I sensed You being always present
When I was hit with anger and hard
By many ills that my energy took and spent.

You directed my eyes to the cross,
To Your great sacrifice, to Your great love
Which shows to all of us, the heavy cost
Of Your love and forgiveness from above.

I came to You, a wounded soul,
Bruised by the waves and tested.
Because Your name is Counselor, Wonderful,
And truly in You I found mercy.

I saw in this sick and dark world
A lot of injustice and hopelessness
A lot of bitterness, just as You told
And much exalted unrighteousness.

You sent me all kinds struggles and pain,
And loss of power and strength
That my entire burden may be at the cross lain
With my groans and their depth.

In You I found all that I need,
Joy, blessed peace, abundant life.
You received me when I was grieved,
Divine Savior, and calmed my strife.

You are the great Shepherd
Who takes care of all of us;
In You, I found treasures,
Grace, and mercy that my life impact.

You say in Your precious Word
That joy is not found on earth,
But only in Your Holy Word,
Which gives us the second birth.

You tell us to rejoice in knowing You
Because our names, which in Your book are written
Are chosen from the world since we became new
That we may adore You forever.

We give You glory, and worshiping,
We thank and wait on You and Your grace
We raise our prayers, our hearts bringing
Praises, desiring Your truth to embrace.

We desire, Lord Jesus, for You to come soon
And to keep our thoughts focused on You
May our hearts and mind be tuned
Towards You, our King Who makes everything new.

December 9, 2008

Searches

With tears and faith,
I come to You, to victory,
And in my great distress
I bring You my poor being.

In my suffering I saw You
And I trusted in You for my salvation
Because You paid a great price,
For my soul's redemption.

Then You searched me out
And You showed me, divine Lamb
That before You, I can bow
Knowing that everything will be well.

You showed me what repentance is,
Which along with faith,
Can move mountains of pain
With Your wonderful grace.

Before You, doubt disappears,
Unbelief and doubt depart,
But Your assurance my soul repairs
And binds my heart.

I looked to You from the valley
And I saw You shining;
And You led me on the way
With my eyes on You aiming.

I felt Your great power
Which took away my pain,
Helped me hide in You, my Tower,
And cleansed me, to my gain.

Great trials have come
But with You I overcame all;
I learned that You are faithful
To an obedient and fearing soul.

I learned to look to You
And not to trust in myself,
To call You to my aid,
Just as You have said.

December 9, 2008

PEACE

"Peace I leave with you, My peace I give to you; not as the world gives do I give you. Let not your heart be troubled, neither let it be afraid."

John 14:27

You, Lord, promised us peace
In this world of great strife and sin.
You gathered us and gave us release;
With Your hand You caught us and brought us in.

You told us not to trouble ourselves
To be courageous and not to be afraid;
But help us, oh precious Jesus,
To trust in You, considering the price You paid.

We are hit seriously from all sides,
And having our eyes focused on You,
You pronounce peace and Your light
And then the storm is subdued.

What overwhelming power,
What authority is in You, Jesus!
In You we are able, every hour,
To walk with Your good news.

Victory You gave us,
You, the King of the heart.
Victory You leave with us,
Which takes us to Paradise.

I need You, I need Your might
And in every moment I desire
To serve You with my life.

To You I come, looking upward,
And I found out that You love me
Because thus says Your precious Word
And You give me new life full of stability

"Peace," You spoke to me,
And only from You have I received it;
Joy, hope, power and authority
You have given me when I believed.

December 10, 2008

The Way, the Truth, the Life

Jesus said to him, "I am the way, the truth, and the life."

John 14:6

You are the only way
And You told us to walk on it:
The narrow and good way
That leads us not astray.

You are the great truth,
And in Your presence all evil
Departs and disappears
With great speed.

You are the abundant life;
You dissipate the fog and shame
And put an end to strife,
Giving me a new name.

You are the great light,
You are the divine revelation;
You are the One who pierce the night
You are worthy of glorification.

You are the Savior,
The Shepherd of my soul:
The good and just Shepherd
Who keeps me from fall.

You help me to reach the shore,
Coming from such a deserted place;
And brought light to my mind and my soul.
Showing me Your marvelous grace

To my wonder, on my path
The Lord showed Himself to me
He kept me away from wrath
And He encouraged me.

December 10, 2008

You Forsook, You Left, You Came

You left the glory of heaven
And You came to this earth
To bring us Your salvation
According to Your Holy Word.

You left the heavenly glory
For earthly confusion and filth;
You came as a fragile Baby
To take away our guilt.

You came to those that took Your name
But they did not want to know You;
Through the valleys of life, they bore shame
And they have fallen, because they forsaken You.

But to those who received You
You gave them redemption
And thus they all became
A chosen and beloved nation.

A chosen people, a royal priesthood
And with Your peaceful voice
You declared them Your children, who
Received from You peace and joy.

December 10, 2008

The Light of Life

You are the light of life
And You call me to You,
You tell me, "Do not be afraid."
To become whole and new.

Your light dissipates the darkness,
Which is around me with its absence of love;
Your light, Jesus, with Your meekness,
Attracts me to the place from above.

Since You enlightened my eyes
You made my soul clean;
In You I found peace and joy that is nice
Which did not disappoint me.

I put my trust and hope in You,
In Your power and victory;
Through faith I came to You,
Preparing me for Your glory.

You opened up my eyes to see what I did not see,
My mind to know what I did not know,
In my heart to feel what I did not feel,
Thus in You I became white as snow.

The price that You paid
Was unspeakably terrible,
For with it, I know that You made
My salvation possible.

For everything, I thank You,
And I want to be for a use,
I desire to serve You and be with You
In Your kingdom – Christ Jesus.

December 17, 2008

LORD, YOU LOVED US

Lord, You have loved us
And that is why You came to earth;
And in a humble, poor place
Was Your holy, miraculous birth.

You left the glory of heaven
To bring the solution to our ego;
And You gave us determination
And to walk and Your Word to sow.

You gave us a purpose in living,
A clear and precise direction
New thoughts, a new way of speaking,
Which to us brings the needed correction.

From the beginning You chose us
To belong entirely to You,
And from this world You picked us
To walk with the ones that are among the few.

You told us to live for You, to believe,
To do good in Your powerful name,
To love, to be compassionate and to forgive,
And to proclaim You without shame.

I saw You up on the cross,
How You gave up Your life
And suffered a great loss,
But You blessed me in my strife.

December 18, 2008

FOR MARY, MY DAUGHTER

The Lord gave you to me
To be my daughter,
And also He has shown to me
His love and His care.

He gifted you in many ways
And also helped you to climb
To arrive high above, that you may
Experience more of His love.

You were and are a ray of light
Who warmed our life, with joy and responsibility,
With your sensitivity, our souls you delight,
And you filled our life with your wit.

You brought us joy that made us ponder,
You helped us to see your ability
To make us see beauty and wonder,
And a life spent with you in humility.

I sowed in your tender soul
The love of God, the Savior;
And in His grace, resoundingly
You responded to His voice.

Others watered the scattered seed,
And it grew deeply and wonderfully;
And in the time of great need
It bore the proper fruit miraculously.

I watch you now as a flower,
Beautiful and fragrant,
Which still grows with power,
Being rooted in the Rock.

I know your aspirations
Your desire to penetrate minds
And I see your determination
To be salt and to spread light.

December 21 2008

For David, my Son

With joy I received you
Into the world when you came;
I cared for you and loved you,
And to God I looked, praising His name.

I taught you to look upward to God
And thus always, to remember
On the path of life, to overcome.
Thru His great power.

Since you were a child,
I observed in you a humble spirit
And a great joy, a nice smile
Which from the Lord, you received it.

You grew up strong and beautifully
Under Christ' s protection,
And then you took Him confidently
As your Savior, giving you a new direction.

Your smile and your good will,
Along with your confidence and faith,
Helped many in good health or ill
To find God's amazing grace.

You were and are a sun beam;
You grew robust and solid
And you filled our lives, like a stream
With love and joy that you received.

You proved to be indeed
A good brother for your sister,
Helping her in her time of need.

I desire that both of you would know
How much you are loved, and I want you to form
A friendship in times both high and low
And also in the time of storm.

May you help each other
And both enjoy the blessings
In the present time and farther
By having clean hearts by God's power.

I want you to remain with integrity,
With joy, humility and kindness;
And rooted in Jesus, with dignity,
To remain on the path of righteousness.

I enjoyed to give you my care and attention,
Because you make me know
That I am in need of courage and determination
And in Him to continue to grow.

December 23, 2008

TOWARDS YOU I RUN

Towards You I run, just as I am,
Because You receive me;
And from my path, oh divine Lamb,
You guide me to Yourself, and make me see.

You direct my steps along Your path
And in You I find blessing and light
My eyes I raise towards Your love
And thus in You I find delight.

When doubts and thoughts press me
And my soul is deeply distressed,
And when the pain does not leave me,
I come to You, because in You I am blessed.

In You I found peace and great joy,
Power, confidence and strength
Because You gave me love,
And hope and life in all its depth.

Hope that doesn't deceive
You put in my troubled soul,
Which heals me of every illness,
Looking to You, Jesus, my Lord.

And yet in me I have limitations and weakness
When I wait for Your wonders to be known,
To be manifested in my life' brokenness
Such way that Your power would be shown.

Increase my faith in You, o, Lord
And help me to look to You all of my days,
Help me to live according to Your Word
And to bring to You my soul's praise

Help me to make Your presence
My life's greatest asset,
And Your sacrifice on the cross
The place where my heart is led.

There is the place where You died,
There is the place where You said "It is finished"
And also there is the place where You cried,
And thus salvation was completed.

Then in the tomb You were laid,
And with a great stone the grave was closed;
And to many You showed Yourself.
When in the third day You powerfully rose,

The same power of resurrection
We see today in the lives of those,
Who with humility, confession,
And repentance, Your invitation chose.

In vain there were guards and the tomb was sealed:
Because the Lord is powerful and great –
He who by His word created the world
Rose triumphantly from the dead.

Jesus Christ is His name –
The One who has dominion over the world,
Our Savior is the same.
The Creator, just as He has told,

December 30, 2008

I Want to Concentrate on You

I want to concentrate on You
And to bless You for who You are
Because You loved me and made me new
And You saved my soul and set me apart.

In You I put my hope and trust and to You I pray
Because through Your Word You told me
That my sins are forgiven, they are cast away
And that I am set aside by You and I am free.

Lord, when I see Your bruised face
At the cross of Golgotha,
I thank You for Your marvelous grace
And help me to give You all my love.

January 11, 2009

In Your Grace

" 'And you shall love the Lord your God with all your heart, with all your soul, with all your mind, and with all your strength.' "

Mark 12:30

Lord, in Your wonderful grace
You gave me the greatest gift,
To be able to bring You praise
And Your name to lift,

I read in Your precious, eternal Word
That only You are the One who is Holy,
And You told us to love You our Lord
With our heart, strength, mind; to love You wholly.

That thus living in You and with You
We may learn to do only good,
To help those around us to know You
To use Your Word as their spiritual food.

You said that living in You and Your grace,
And with You living in us,
We will be able to see Your face.
We will have divine life that will last.

January 15, 2009

I Want in my Life

I want in this life of mine
For You to be my guide –
To protect and to preserve me,
And on my way to accompany me.

To walk with me through the valleys,
Even when I have to pass through trials
To climb on the mountains and on the hills,
And to go with me through my life's ills.

To feel Your presence close
And along to consider all loss,
To go through the storms of life
And You to be my constant guide.

You are my great help,
Guide and Protector,
The source of great joy and light
On the path of my earthly life.

You are my support and guide –
You, who are the Rock tested and tried–
Fortress in troubled times,
For Your love and faithfulness shines.

You are the cornerstone,
You are the Son of Man,
Who with sacrifice supreme
Came to us to bring us in.

You shed Your blood
And Your body was torn;
You washed away our sins
And made us clean.

Clean, saved, and wonderful
On the cross You made us powerful
And when we received You
You transformed us and made us new.

And You made us whiter than snow,
Thus You made us know
The guilt that contained us
In the sea of forgiveness was cast.

January 16, 2009

THE CROSS

I learned that Your cross
Is the road that leads
Up there to Golgotha, the place
Where I can see Your face.

You were hurt and wounded for me,
You gave Your life to make me free,
To change the direction of my gaze
Towards Your salvation and grace.

You told us to take a loss,
So that we can carry our cross,
To walk on the way that leads us
To see our two natures.

Looking at the cross we can see
The costly price that made us free.
The obedience and the love
Which, together came from above.

Our nature desires at its core
To control us and to grow more and more,
They want our life to master,
Leading us to great disaster.

Then, when again we looked at the cross,
And the new nature with power guides us
A new nature we are given when we believed.
Which wars with the old one which is deceived

The cross brings us forgiveness,
Love, reconciliation and righteousness
The renunciation of what is evil, and restoration,
You Jesus bring us Your salvation.

The cross is hard to carry
Help us to advance on the path, not to tarry
And that is why we always ask You,
To help us to remain faithful to You.

On the cross You satisfied God's wrath
And it shows us the narrow path,
Where our hearts become clean
Free from confusion, free from guilt.

You told us to carry our cross
And on the path slowly to advance,
To look at You as our leader, Savior and Lord
To overcome any evil thru the power of Your Word.

January 17, 2009

WISDOM

The fear of the Lord is the beginning of wisdom.

Proverbs 9:10

The joy of the Lord is our strength;
It keeps us strong in trials of life
When we walk upon our ways
And it confronts our selfish pride.

In the trials of life, for each single situation
We need Your wisdom, to be able to live
Humbly under Your protection.

We need Your wisdom each and every day
To free us from evil and from difficulty
And to remain with us always,

To protect us from all kinds of temptations,
Which cling strongly to our lives;
To give us Your precious salvation
And to serve as our necessary guide.

Wisdom protects us against wickedness
And on our way it accompanies us;
The fear of You, Lord, leads us to righteousness
And is what encourages us.

Wisdom leads us to righteous living
It helps us to live in safety
And offers to the soul cleansing;
And gives us true hope aplenty.

The fear of the Lord protects and defends
And I want it in my mind and my soul,
His wisdom, my life corrects
Frees me and makes me whole.

Through wisdom You created the world,
And also through it You formed the man;
From the dust of the ground You took him
And You gave Him, Your holy breath.

Through wisdom, You came to the earth
Because You loved us, so much
Also through wisdom You gave us life,
And redeemed us from all evil with Your touch

Wisdom gave herself in our place
Wisdom came and the world did not know it
Wisdom cried on the cross giving us grace
And thus our salvation was finished.

Wisdom declared that all was well done
That all was well arranged, just as told –
That the universe came into being
Through His pronounced Word.

January 18, 2009

THE ELECTION

The world is in much confusion
And believes such an illusion:
That a man is her hope, and her deliverance –
His thinking and his performance.

We live in difficult times, the times of the end –
When many evils happen, that offend
Those who want to live according to Your word
And to follow You, Lord.

This man chosen through ignorance
Presents a false assurance
Because the truth is considered not good
And like garbage is trampled underfoot.

Many people put blindly their hope in him
And refused to trust in You, Jesus –
That only You are the blessed Truth, that release
That many desire in their search for peace.

This man is seen as a Messiah,
And to him is shown all joy,
But he is not what he is believed to be,
And thus through him the world is deceived.

The way to You is getting narrower all the more,
And we ask You now, like before
To help us and to strengthen us on our journey
As we live with You day to day.

The defamations and persecution will come,
But we ask Him power to overcome
When persecution of all sorts and of all kinds,
In our way will arrive with their blinds.

Help us, Lord Jesus be gracious and merciful
Help us to remain all our lives faithful
And help us to bring to the altar
Our gifts, and praises from afar.

The gift of faith that You gave us
And which through Your power transformed us –
May it remain clean and unaltered,
Offered to You, Wonderful Savior.

The gift of fervent love, the gift of suffering –
The gift of our devotion, the gift of loving,
That You gave to us to be able to share
Showing to others Your care.

The gift of faith, expressed in our weakness
Along with the gift of trust and the gift of praise
The gift of our clean lives, and sacrifices
The proof of Your wonderful power in us.

January 20, 2009

YOUR CREATION

Lord, when I look at Your creation
I see Your wisdom and Your mighty hand–
I see how You created the sun and the moon
And all that is in the sky, in water and on land

You gave them laws of functionality
And You gave them a special place,
You created the stars and gave them stability
And You call all of them by name.

You created them through Your Word
To give light to this earth, day and night
And all that is in the world
You created by Your might.

During the day, the sun gives us its light,
And in the night the moon lights our path,
And all these bring to our sight
The great proof of Your truth and love.

But with grief, I have to hear
From the man, who is Your creation,
That all appeared at random,
Thus denying Your contribution.

All kinds of explanations they give
For all that You have created
And Your word they don't want to receive.

They invented a story that is not true,
A story that is founded on evolution-
They deny the credit that is due
To You, the author of creation.

The world is enslaved by diverse actions
That come from all kinds of foolish passions
And does not see nature adorned
With Your good works, oh, Lord

Those who do not have You as their shelter
Worship what You have made and is permanent
For this reason, they do not know any better
And they deny what is clear and evident.

You created man in Your image and likeness
Above all the other creatures, that roam
And for him You died, to give him forgiveness
That through You, he may arrive home.

January 27, 2009

THE INVITATION

He is extending you today
His invitation to come to Him
And He wants You to obey
Towards His good and loving will.

He is calling you, "Come;"
Do not delay to respond,
He widely opens His arms
For He wants with you to bond,

When you are on the path of life,
For now, for the present time, come just as you are
He wants you to save you from your strife.

Come quickly and do not delay,
Come and you will have forgiveness,
And He will take your hand on the way
And change the direction of your gaze.

He will show you the road that leads
To Golgotha, to the place where was His cross,
And He will show you the price that was paid
With a great sacrifice at such a high cost

He will help you to understand
That not through traditions and laws
Can you come to be freed
From the sin of unbelief and all your flaws.

The road of the cross leads you up above
And only thus you will be able to see
The place where Jesus's powerful love,
Was shown clearly to you and me.

This invitation is still made to all,
To all those who will listen –
To come with their hurt souls
To receive peace and rest.

This invitation is offering you a new life
So that in your heart you may have
Streams of living water, and light
And you will be full with the desire to serve.

He invites you to receive His gift,
Given to you only through grace,
The gift of the His Holy Spirit –
To guide you in this earthly race.

January 31, 2009

There is Much Power in Your Blood

There is much power in Your blood,
Which flows from Your torn body
Because You loved us, so much
And with a high price You saved us.

Our sin had such a high cost,
That You suffered unspeakable pain
When You died on the cross,
Our lives to touch, to our gain.

And thru Your death You won for Yourself
A great people, thus freed from sin;
And in Your freedom, we entered,
And You gave us Your Holy Spirit.

You guide us in this earthly life
And in the world You are our Counselor;
You help us and You strengthens us
And in life You lead us, for You are our Leader.

Through Your resurrection You overcame death,
And now we know that You are alive;
We come to You because from great depth
You took us with Your might.

From depths of pain You took us,
From a hard and rocky road,
And gave us light, peace, and mercy
Carrying our heavy load.

Through holy prayers we come
To enter into Your holy presence
We come to You, divine Lamb,
With much perseverance.

Faith comes through hearing
Your Holy and powerful Word
Because only it can bring
Salvation to the entire world.

If with our mouth we confess before men
That Jesus Christ is Lord who gives us redemption
And if we believe that God resurrected Him,
Then we will find our souls' salvation.

February 6, 2009

THE CRUCIFIXION

You, Lord, did only good
While being on this earth;
You did wonders that the world saw-
Your deeds were enabled by Your Word.

You opened the eyes of the blind
And gave hearing to the deaf,
And with Your voice You told them
To trust in You, and You healed them.

Then You resurrected the dead,
And You healed the lepers,
But only one returned to You
To thank You for making him new.

But those from the upper class,
Those of high rank, did not receive You,
And from among them, some said
That too many towards You are led.

Then they provoked the crowd
And they advised all who were present
To ask that You be judged,
And by Pilate to be charged.

One of those chosen by You
Forsook You and ran to the priests,
Asking them what would they give
If he would hand You to them .

But before, all this, You, Lord, prayed
To the Father that if it were possible,
This cup of bitter venom indignation
To pass from His serious consideration.

And with cold sweat of blood
You called Him, patiently waiting,
And soon after, for all our sin,
You, Jesus, cried for the cup was filled

And yet there was no other solution:
Jesus had to bear our sins on the cross
Set between two thieves, He who is the King
Was forsaken even by those who in Him believed.

Only His mother watched Him,
Having John standing beside her,
When Jesus cried from the cross,
Giving His life at such a high cost.

From the cross Jesus cried of thirst,
And then someone gave to Him
A sponge in vinegar soaked,
Which He refused to receive it.

And when on the cross He died,
They pierced His side with a sword,
And from it immediately gushed out
The blood mixed with water.

Then from the cross with a loud voice He cried,
"My God, My God, why have You forsaken Me?"
And thus He gave up His spirit
For the sinners who He loved indeed.

And after that great price was paid,
Through the supreme sacrifice brought by Him,
One of the soldiers pronounced
That "truly He is the Son of God" – Christ Jesus.

Why so much hatred I asked?
Why, with their mouths
Did they ask for Him to be crucified,
When He loved them so much?

There at the cross Love and hatred met:
Love was praying for forgiveness;
Hatred did not want a Savior,
And, momentarily, it won.

Then He declared that all was finished,
That salvation was fully accomplished,
That the ones who believe are redeemed,
And that by Him, they are all received.

He came to show us the new way
Which opens for us from this moment on:
A narrow, difficult and a tried way,
But the one that His love conveys.

February 7, 2009

WHAT IS TRUTH?

When Your were brought to Pilate
And he saw You, in front of him
He asked You who you are
Wondering if You were the King.

But at first You did not respond,
And yet later with authority You told him
That it is true, he said it right
And that the Father revealed it to him.

Then Pilate asked Jesus again
 "What is truth?" he inquired
Because in himself there was struggle
And between good and evil he was entangled.

Although he did not find You guilty,
Desiring to reconcile the crowd
He exposed You again, hurt and bruised
Before of the world that saw You being abused

And he told them to beat You more
And then to carry You
To the Golgotha, where his mob
Drained You of precious life.

There, on the hill of Golgotha,
You gave Your own life;
This was the our invitation
To the road that brings us salvation.

What is truth? You ask.
It is the power that destroys evil;
Is the person of Jesus and His word
That attracts us who believe, upward.

Pilate washed his hands,
Thinking that he freed himself of guilt,
But when Jesus died with authority
He was struck by the reality.

And to quiet the crowd, Pilate
Put above the cross a sign
On it was written: "This is The King of the Jews" –
He was the One who embodies all the Truth.

Then in a new tomb they laid You,
They sealed it, and commanded many guards
To watch it continuously, not to leave it alone
Closing it with a heavy stone

And the You showed Yourself to many;
The mark of the nails they saw,
When on the third day You resurrected
And thus, even Thomas believed.

O, help me Lord, I ask
In my life and in my heart
To remain close to You,
To worship before You.

February 9, 2009

You, Jesus, and the World

"Lord, to whom shall we go? You have the words of eternal life."

John 6:68

"I am the vine, you are the branches. He who abides in Me, and I in him, bears much fruit; for without Me you can do nothing."

John 15:5

You, Jesus, told us holy words.
The world imposed on us its thinking.
You helped us on our road
The world stained us with its way of living.

You gave us Your life abundant
You reconciled us with the Father;
You offered us Your great love
And Your salvation we share.

You called us to hope and rest,
To quietness, peace, and light,
You prepared for us what is best
If we will look to You, for insight.

You are the vine, we are the branches
And our life comes from You;
Without You, we can do nothing.

You are our shelter and our souls' protector;
Prince of peace, the One who watches over us,
Our leader and our guide, our provider
You are the Bright Morning Star,

The world's desire is to separate us from You
And to impart to us from its pleasures,
But You call us to Yourself,
You want us to be Your treasure.

You offer us Your love, truth and salvation;
The world gives us nothing satisfactory,
You give us abundant life, redemption
And You want to free us from sin's slavery.

February 26, 2009

THE FRUIT OF THE SPIRIT

Gal 5:22-25

The fruit of the Holy Spirit
We obtain through Jesus' sacrifice
When we come to Him
Whom our soul glorifies.

It is given to us as a gift
And through His grace,
Love and joy we receive
Along with peace, and meekness.

Then the doing of what is good
We learn from Your word –
Strength and meekness, too
Along with self- control .

Against these things
There is no law that can act
And all these good things
Will help us, will put us apart.

Thus let us live in the Spirit
And let us be content and joyful
That we no longer pursue empty glory,
And no longer we will be anxious.

Living daily on this earth
Through the power of the Holy Spirit,
We become new creations –
Full of life and energetic.

Halleluiah, glory to You, oh, Lord
For soon Your kingdom will come
We will see You, just as You have told
When we will enter into the city from above.

February 10, 2009

THE TESTED ROCK

You are my solid Rock on which I stand
You, with Your deep love protects me
You shelter me from evil and my knees I bend
Before You with an attitude of humility.

You are the tested Rock from long ago–
Remaining through the storms, solid and unmoving –
You are the only salvation for my stressed soul.
When the boisterous wind blows and the sky is darkening,

You remain the same yesterday, today and tomorrow
You are my only model of a life with integrity,
Of a life full of faithfulness and love mingled with sorrow,
Of a life of sacrifice, a life lived in humility.

You, Jesus, protected me each single day
And from many evils You saved me;
When difficult waves crashed over me in every way
And bruised me and hurt me powerfully.

They hurt me but they did not overwhelm me
Because You came down to my aid;
You took my strife and gave me stability
And You fulfilled all that You said.

This Rock is Jesus Christ –
The name that is the most beautiful of all,
The name that heals any pain,
The name that has the greatest power of all.

February 11, *2009*

MORE, LORD

More, Lord, of You I desire
To look at You, for salvation
To be with You and to be near
Lord, I need Your compassion:

To look at Your deep beauty
And to see Your meekness;
To feel Your love and purity
And in trials to sense Your closeness

I want You to search my heart
And to cleanse it from sin;
Then, I ask You, Lord, to be my part
And on You I want to lean.

More may I to give to You
For the life that You have changed in me
And more may I thank You
For the salvation that You gave me.

More time with You I want to spend
And less with me and my interests
More I want Your will to understand
And more I desire Your name to bless.

More I want to follow You on this journey
Upon Your path I want to walk towards eternity
The path of trials is the path that leads to the way
Of many renunciations, the way of integrity.

February 22, 2009

FORGIVENESS

You gave me forgiveness in Your great love-
And through Your grace You brought me redemption
For my sin that was ugly and dark
And You gave me the gift of salvation.

You promised us forgiveness and total healing
When You called us, You gave us the right
To become Your children who bring
Praises to our Lord the King.

Our forgiveness cost You so much
Your life, given was all You could do
On the cross of Golgotha, to touch
Our lives and minds and souls too.

Forgiveness for hatred that was shown
Which separated from us the dross of sin,
Shows us how to love His own
And together to look above to Him.

Offering us Your forgiveness,
You gave us a great responsibility:
For us to desire goodness and kindness
And to be lovers of mankind;

To respond with good for evil
And thus to praise Your name,
To bless our enemies with much or little
And to sing to You, for You took our shame.

I thank You that through Your forgiveness
I have known Your liberty,
I learned meekness and kindness
For You gave me stability.

Your act of intervention in my day to day life
Brings truth, light, clarity, power and healing
Of deep and untold hurts that bite
Which our souls are subject to receiving.

You told us to forgive as You forgave us
And not to forget that this is a commend;
We should remember that what we sow will follow us
We soon will reap what we spread.

February 22, 2009

WHY ME?

From far away, from strange paths,
You, Lord, call me to Yourself,
And I ask myself, "Why me?"

Why have You chosen me from this world?
From the world You brought me into Your fold
You showed me Your mercy and Your grace
When You forgave me so, that I can bring You praise

Why did You choose to save me,
To do good and to bless me,
When many times I annoyed You
And with my thoughts I forgot You?

Reading Your Word, I found out
That from my mother's womb
You predestinated me from the start
You selected me and set me apart.

Not because I deserved it, or did anything
But because You proposed to give me everything
You desire that this living soul
Be obedient to You in all.

I thank You Lord Jesus, for Your great love;
You showed me direction from above,
For You had mercy even on me,
And You filled my soul with peace.

February 23, 2009

BEFORE YOU

Before You, before Your Majesty
We all will stand in awe
To receive our reward.

And then, when the books will be opened
And the names will be read,
Those who will be called by name
Will be with Him- there will be no shame.

Our lives will be evaluated according to Your Word
And our thoughts and words heard afterwards
Our deeds uncovered, revealed before Him
Then the decision will be pronounced by the King.

Some will be with You in eternity that You prepared
And with Your angels, they will rejoice forever
And others will be far away from Your presence
Meeting pain and hatred and resistance.

A body of glory You will give us
In heaven when we'll find ourselves there;
A body of eternity, a body of glory
Offered to us with great joy.

There, pain, fear, and death will be no more;
There, joy will be in abundance for evermore
And the trouble of earth will be gone
For we will see Jesus on His throne.

February 24, 2009

When the Ship of my Life...

When the ship of my life through waves floats
And when I put my hope in arriving ashore,
The storm comes and the wind howls,
And the sails of my ship are thorn.

Then when fears press me
And when doubts come,
When all strength leaves me,
Divine Savior, to You, I run.

And when I am with You
I feel Your embrace with love;
Peace surrounds me, my soul renews
Joy overwhelms me, and I am calm.

I feel the protection that is around me
Like at the first time when You gave it to me
It strengthens me and keeps me,
And I do not feel the storm when it strikes.

Then, when the storm calms down, Lord
And when the clouds dissipate at Your word
The beautiful sun rises majestic and high
Revives us and it clears up the sky.

Then, in that untold and peaceful beauty,
I can see well the power from above:
The power that revived me and helped me
The power of Your great love.

That power from above
Is only in You, Jesus,
Who came down to us –
Bringing us the good news

In Him anchor yourself and remain steadfast
And in Him place your trust,
So that you may arrive undefiled
In the place preserved for His own.

That is the most beautiful place,
The most precious and most valued:
A place of light and brightness,
A place full of eternal love.

There, fears, pain, trials, and death will be no more;
There, all will be holy and glorious
Clean, and wonderful, for we will be with the Savior
And with the Father all will be reconciled.

There His glory will shine forever
And there will be no need of light;
Time will no more exists, ever
Because eternity will persist along with His might.

There we will meet with all the ones –
From all nations – but all redeemed
And with the same price won

On streets of gold we will walk,
An eternal dwelling we will have there
And from the throne of mercy will flow
Life and love under His care.

February 24, 2009

In This Jar of Clay

2 Corinthians 4:7

In this jar of clay made by Your hands
Lord, You could hide Your treasure
You put in it so much richness, helping it to stand
The thought towards eternity that has no measure.

In this jar of clay You put complexity
You gave to it such an important role;
You put Your image in it and gave it authority
To teach, to love and made it whole

In this jar of clay You put much ability
You put an eternal soul for a purpose,
Soul, which You saved from hell by Your authority.

And in this jar of clay You put will and determination
Many emotions and feelings along with conscience
Soul, to which You gave expression through Your salvation
And through thoughts brought to Your cross.

Then, to this jar of clay You gave a mind
To be able to think, and to understand
And to learn to thank You for being so kind
Willing in Your presence to stand.

Breath of life You gave to this jar of clay,
And our souls receive strength to live
Became active and in great need to pray
And were with us having power to believe.

You knew this jar of clay that was going away
And that's why You formed a plan,
You gave Your Son just as Your Word says.

CRUSHED

The Lord is near to those who have a broken heart,
And saves such as have a contrite spirit.

–Psalm 34:18

Lord, You called us to believe,
To come to Your salvation,
And You told us to receive
Your personal invitation.

I came to You with a contrite spirit
With my hurt and bruised soul
And You received me just as I was
And healed me and made me whole.

You rebuke those who are proud and the boastful
But You receive those who have a contrite spirit
Because they look to You and are worshipful.

You are near to those with a broken heart
Because they have a holy calling,
And those with a contrite spirit, You set apart
Because in You they are rejoicing.

March 1, 2009

WORSHIPFULLY

Worshipfully, Lord, I come to You
From foreign paths and difficult paths
To see Your brightness and to be renewed
Because I need Your powerful love.

With humility and through faith
I desire Your victory in every situation
And with all my life and strength
I ask for Your salvation.

In my life I want to ask
Your power to take being
So that others will be blessed by
My devotion in deed and thinking

With love and reverence I adore You –
Because You are my Savior,
Who brought me freedom, joy, hope,
Peace and forgiveness like I never had before

I found in You balance for my life
When I raised my thoughts towards You;
You placed me on Your side,
Showing to me Your truth.

Worshipfully I desire my life to bring
To sit to Your feet with my all
To prostrate myself with my being
And to bring to You my eternal soul.

Come therefore, soul, propose
That you will serve Him worshipfully,
That you will respond to His call,
That you will live with Him joyfully

On the narrow path of faith
Come and taste His truth and love
To see how good He is – to have His grace
Jesus Christ, who is from above.

"The young lions lack and suffer hunger,
But those who seek the Lord
Shall not lack any good thing," but rather
They love Your precious Word.

March 6, 2009

IN YOUR GREAT PLAN

In Your great plan to save us
You sent Your only begotten Son
So that the world may clearly see
Your love through and receive it.

In Your great plan to bring us closer to You
You redeemed us all with no restriction
With the same price, that was not new
Shed blood- that brought us salvation.

In Your plan You chose from each generation
From the world You picked us, Your Word to proclaim
To follow You from each nation
And to sing to You, praising Your name.

Your blood shed at Golgotha' mountain
Proved Your love to be true
For us sinful ones to claim–
That we who believe, belong to You.

In Your great plan You called us to repentance
To come to You with a contrite spirit
You lighted our path as an evidence
That You want us to follow You in humility.

In Your great plan, You, Jesus, came
Because You loved us, Your creation,
And You helped us to understand
The path we have to take to redemption.

March 8, 2009

FROM THE VALLEY

I cried to You from the valley from were I was
You listened and payed attention to my voice;
You came to me and lifted me up
Gave me joy and set me apart.

You reached me from where I was
In trials you guided me to understand their purpose
And You helped me to climb the mountain of life,
Seeing the beauty in the cruel valley where I cried.

There in the valley, many tears I shed;
Many hurts and fears surrounded me,
And my wounded soul was left
With many scars, bruised and hurt.

As long as I continued to keep quiet,
As long as I looked downward, I felt tired
And as long as I lived pleasing my ego's claim
I found myself all the more low and in profound pain.

But with all this I had to experiment,
So that I'll look to You and on You to depend
To work at patience, confidence, strength, and trust,
Along with repentance for my present and past.

There on the mountain my soul was brought
To the place where You, Jesus fought
For my sin and where You suffered and died
So that the wrath of the Father would be satisfied.

Thus I should remain tried and humble,
Not delaying to put my gaze upon You,
And to remember that for me You died
Because You loved me so much.

You brought me healing and stability
And in my soul You put hope and much ability
Today, with gratitude I come to thank You,
And with humility I want to serve You.

March 8, 2009

SPRING

Winter passed, the earth warmed up,
The flowers started to appear,
And nature is all revived
Because it is spring here.

The sky is blue, the nature is quiet,
And the sun is beautiful and bright;
And, I, a traveler, gazing around
Look at the work of Your might

The birds fly and sing
And even the broken reed
Still remains strong,
And nothing seems to be wrong.

Everything is revived
Coming out of the cold winter
The beauty of nature encourages us
And our desire for life is awakened.

The earth accumulated much water;
With rain and sun You endowed it.
Much snow also You gave to it,
And thus the seeds sprouted.

Oh, spring, oh, spring, you
Make everything look like new;
You are the season that makes us feel regenerated
Transformed within and invigorated.

Flowers of all colors and forms
Decorate the landscape that surrounds us,
Making our lives more pleasant.

The trees bloomed and the grass is green,
Reviving even the broken heart
Bringing much refreshment,
Along with hope and encouragement.

You, Lord, offer us the spring season of our souls;
You renew our minds like for the first time,
Giving us peace and joy and righteousness
Along with love, hope, and tenderness.

March 14, 2009

FREEDOM

You brought us freedom
In Your great love –
Freedom from the sin
Which we found ourselves in.

Freedom from oppression,
Freedom from torment and obsession,
Freedom to come to You,
Freedom to be renewed

You gave us the freedom to choose,
And to not be under the law anymore –
Freedom to be under Your grace,
Which is a great gift in our life's race.

Freedom of expression
You gave us while we are on this earth –
Freedom of thinking,
Freedom of speaking;

Freedom of action,
And thus, to see Your wonder;
Freedom to look upward
To You, Jesus, and to Your power.

But our precious freedom
Cost You everything,
For You had to take the venom of all
Of our burdened souls.

You gave Your life
When You were mocked and whipped
You gave it as a supreme sacrifice of love
So that we could be received above.

Our liberty has a great price,
A price of untold value:
A price of redemption,
A price of salvation

Our liberty, won with blood,
Shows us Your profound love for us
And makes us respond in the same way,
With love and reverence, we pray

This freedom, this liberty
Gives us a great responsibility:
To live for His glory from birth
And as long as we are on this earth.

Let us bring Him honor and praise,
And from Him, let us learn
How to walk on the path of life.
And how to raise His name on high,

March 17, 2009

WHEN I LOOK TO YOU

They looked to Him and were radiant,
And their faces were not ashamed.

Psalm 34:5

When I look to You
My face is not full of shame,
But rather my heart is quiet
Because I am watched by You.

When I look to You
The enemy becomes powerless
Because Your blessing
Heals my wounds.

When I look to You, You strengthen me,
You remind me that You love me,
You give light to my life,
And You bless me.

When I look to You, my soul fills
With hope, peace, and joy
Because I know that all will be well
When You come towards me.

When I look to You, everything is clear,
And as reward, I receive as a gift
The cleansing of my heart
And the salvation of my soul.

The gift comes with a great responsibility
Which creates a possibility
For Your visibility
When our lives are tested.

When I look to You, my mind relaxes
Because Your Spirit works
To form me, to perfect me,
And to conform me to Your word.

Without You, I can not live,
Nor can my life develop;
However, when I look to You and talk to You,
My covenant with You comes easy.

Your yoke is not heavy
When on our way we always walk with You;
Your burden is light,
As it was the first time.

March 20, 2009

YOUR PROTECTION

Your love attracts us to Yourself,
And gives us Your blessings,
Puts us under Your protection,
And it changes our direction,

Your protection is of great value:
It protects us from evil and darkness,
Makes our souls strong,
And saves us from Satan's claws.

Your protection is what we desire
And it makes us be stronger
With great passion and stability
Vigilant upon Your path, and free.

Your protection shelters us
And brings blessings to us
It strengthens us with each mile,
And covers us in the hour of trial.

Under Your blood shed on the cross
We truly find protection at Your cost,
Shelter, support in the storm,
And patience when we are in great loss.

At the liberation from Egypt,
You reminded Your people
How much You loved them,
And thus You gave them Your law to observe.

Then You stayed with them and You led them
While their path led towards You;
You brought salvation and love,
And prepared for tem a place with You above.

Through Your sacrifice we received protection
Complete and essential for our redemption
And thus there is no more need to shed any blood
To bring sacrifices, to kill any animal

Your sacrifice, Jesus, is the greatest lesson
By which we may learn true protection –
Protection paid with a great price,
Full of power, and watched by You, Jesus Christ.

March 22, 2009

TOGETHER WITH YOU

Together with You,
When I go through storm,
The trial is lighter
Because Your plan is unfolding.

When I am together with You,
Even if the clouds are thick and they thunder,
You give me rest and peace
Because before You everything quiets.

All fear goes away
Because Your presence in us produces
Confidence and faith,
Prudence and victory.

Then the sun appears,
And with its great brightness
Warms up our lives
And speaks to us of Your kindness.

The greatest sun of life on this earth
Is, Father God, Your Holy Son
Who came as a baby here beneath
And brought us Your Word.

Then You gave to us Your Spirit
To be with us permanently,
You created in us a new being,
And Your Holy Spirit saves us mightily

The wind calms down, the waves retreat,
And all the trials draw me towards You;
I remember that by being together with You
I will obtain the crown of life.

You, Jesus, are the Morning Sun;
You are the source of our life;
You preserve us on the way,
And You help us on our journey.

Together with You, we can take the next step
Because You are our Creator and Protector
You guide us with care and love and give us help
Because You are our Lord and Savior.

But when we take our eyes from You
We are confused and fear- stricken
And we look at the great waves and wind,
We are wounded by many thoughts and concerns.

When we again see the mountains of burdens
Which produce in us great grief,
Help us to remember
That only in You will we conquer and find relief.

Oh, strengthen our trust
Because without You we are empty
And deepen it within us
So, that for You we will be ready.

Help us to live always
Together with You,
That thus the difficulty of life
May be turned into good.

Being together with You
Is my good portion;
And I come to thank You
For Your salvation.

To serve You with my life
Is all that I desire
Along with proclaiming You
Since You took me from the mire.

March 30, 2009

In Every Place

In every place and in all the games,
Through all circles of people and on all paths,
The world searches for You in vain,
But it does not want to receive You as their gain.

In confusion and spiritual blindness
The world speaks about love,
But true love the people do not know,
Because they do not let Your love in their lives to flow.

They do not know that love is
Your whole story, all that involves
A story with a powerful meaning,
A story to be known in hearing and living.

They do not know that love starts
With the generous "agape"
Which performs the supreme sacrifice,
Thus giving all at full price.

They look in all places,
But they avoid the cross
Because there evil was confronted
And Satan was defeated.

There Your love was shown
And it took our sin;
There You, Jesus, paid the great price
When on the cross You were crucified.

There You proclaimed
That the debt was finished,
That all in full is paid,
And thus the Father's plan was fulfilled.

April 5, 2009

On the Way Towards You

On the way towards You, I went upon rocks,
I passed through deep valleys,
And I fell, but You helped me
And with Your hand You raised me.

On the way towards You, I was wounded,
I was hurt and I suffered,
But You, with Your love, strengthened me,
And You helped me see.

On the way towards You, many temptations came
And many times my soul they troubled;
When I took my eyes from You,
My soul was carried away from You.

I accumulated many things –
And they wanted to control me,
I attached myself to them
And that is why I needed Your help.

You reminded me that there is a higher purpose
A deep and wonderful purpose:
For which You created me,
To serve You ceaselessly.

That is why on the way towards You
I need Your deep intervention
So that Your love will bring my life's cleansing
And do its good work in me through Your blessing.

Only through Your Holy Spirit
Can I renounce the things of this earth,
Gain You all the more,
And listen always to You, since my sin You bore.

Help me, Lord, to detach myself from all these things,
Help me to You to cling
And to be able to be a vessel of honor
In Your great work.

On the way towards You, I look at the target,
And when I hurt myself on the rocks,
You, on the way, encourage me
And through each hurt, You teach something to me.

On the way towards You, I learn to look straight ahead
And to listen to Your powerful words;
I learn to wait with patience and expectation
For Your great mercy and for Your salvation.

I learn that on the way towards You
Everything works for good;
I learn that through pain and sorrow
I can come to You today and tomorrow.

On the way towards You, I also learn to help others,
As well as to leave my comfort,
To be able to support in their grief
Those who have need of You as their relief.

Only then will they come to You –
When they are at the limits of their strength;
They also will find themselves on the way towards You,
And towards You, they will have their view.

Then on the way towards You I saw
Many paths of clay:
One was called "Materialism,"
Another was "Idealism."

I also saw the path of "Religion"
Which leads many upon it
To respect laws that have no measure
Created by man from his evil nature.

The path of the "Materialism" was alluring
With many lovely attractions,
But walking on it, you get lost
And you forget about the cross.

Then I met the path of "Humanism"
Which leads to free thinking
And thus in the end denies You as King.

After this, I met the path of "Pleasure"
And showed me enticing offers
Which presented me passing satisfactions
Which plunged me into the depths of reflection.

Then, not too far away, was the path of "Lying" –
The path of hatred and of deceit –
And looking at it, I saw many people walking on it
That truly made me ill.

But walking farther and farther
I saw another path which separated itself from the others:
It was named "Trust and Repentance," it led to glory,
And it was the path of victory.

I wanted to walk upon it,
And I saw a sign above it saying: " Love" –
Love that sacrificed itself for us,
Love sealed with blood.

Then walking on this path
Where I could see mercy and compassion.
I felt the power of Your presence,
For it lead me to forgiveness

On the way towards You, I saw good and evil
And I felt the guidance of Your Spirit,
And thus You, Jesus, guided me
From You, strength I received.

April 12, 2009

AT THE CROSSROADS

When through life I travel
I arrive at the crossroads,
Where many thoughts lead
And come to my head and accompany me

At the crossroads of ideas
And from people of all kinds,
You helped me to choose what is wright
 To be with the ones that are on Your side.

At the crossroads
I stand and with great wonder I look
At all the empty things
Which shallowness brings.

When I stand at the crossroads,
My thoughts bring me
To You, good Lord,
Where I can pour out my soul.

Before you, I prostate myself
And I come to You from sin's abyss,
For You give me direction
And You lead me to Your salvation.

When I am at the crossroads,
I desire Your Holy Word;
I desire Your counsel from Your riches
Which are shown in Your scriptures.

April 15, 2009

HAPPINESS

In this world, happiness is
The grand ideal and the great pursuit
Of those who look only at what is seen
And in Your words do not believe.

For some happiness is to be as high as possible –
On the high peaks, and to have their names visible –
In the sight of everyone
And on the lips of many

Happiness for others
Means to be elevated in their own eyes,
To have things in abundance
And more and more possessions.

But You said, "Blessed are the poor in spirit,
For theirs is the kingdom of heaven,"
With its richness and beauty.

You also said, "Blessed are the meek,
For they will inherit the earth.
Blessed are those who hunger for righteousness,"
For they will be fulfilled and clean in the mind.

The world does not know about mercy,
And does many things out of disgust,
Cruelty, and hatred,
Thus showing its impurity.

Those around me do not know to show mercy,
But only their souls bound
By many false promises,
Yet they are souls which can be saved.

You said that the one who has mercy
Will himself be given mercy,
And thus his cry
Will set him apart for Your blessing.

The ones with clean hearts
Will see God,
And this I desire
In the duration of my life.

Then You said, "Blessed are the peacemakers,
For they shall be called sons of the heavenly Father."
They are receptive and loving,
And they serve You sacrificially.

When persecution comes on account of Your righteousness
Help us to respond with love and meekness,
For You said that the kingdom of God
Belongs to those who look to You by their faith.

You told us to be happy
When we are abused because of You,
Hated by the world,
And all the more disrespected, too.

You said that our reward will be great
And that from You we will have encouragement
On the narrow and difficult path,
Lead by Your tender voice, which is permanent.

Oh Lord, teach us true happiness,
Which has as its foundation total devotion;
Teach us to understand what You desire from us
While You walk with us through life.

Help us to understand that happiness is
Your promise, which comes
When we look to You.

You created us to rejoice
And to take Your Word
Into our minds and our souls,
And it will stay with us, along with Your voice.

You have shown us how to be happy,
But only guided by You
Will we be able to carry You in our thoughts
And follow You.

Happiness is only in You,
In obedience and in doing good deeds;
It is a process of deep growth
Only possible with Your power.

April 20, 2009

THE MUSTARD SEED

If you have faith
As a mustard seed,
You will do away with the bitterness of life,
For you have His might.

Through true faith,
You can tell the mountain of pain
To leave and to let your life be clean
And free from the burden of sin.

At the pronouncement of the name of Jesus
Everything becomes subject to Him,
And by His power
All the evil around us disappears.

He gave us authority,
He encourages our soul,
And our fight He fights,
Bringing completion to our broken lives.

April 20, 2009

Soon

Soon, You, Lord, will come
And we will see You,
And then we will feel Your power again
When with You we reign.

Soon, the trumpet will sound,
You will gather us from all around,
And we will be with You eternally,
Protected by You fully.

Soon our faith
Will be made sight
When You come in Your light
And receive us in Your grace.

Soon all that is seen will pass away,
And with Your power You will create a new world;
Soon we will see the victory, just as You have told,
To which our faith will have brought us all the way

Soon we will be in line
With all the redeemed ones, by Your love divine,
Found by You,
And thus becoming new.

Soon we will see the glory of heaven
And its untold beauty,
And we will be before the throne
Of the great King – Jesus.

There we will walk on the streets of gold
And we will have a dwelling of precious stones;
In Your presence we will be,
And Your face we will see.

We will see the tree of life
And the river of life will flow from Your throne,
And in You we will be strong,
Through the power of Your Word.

Soon, we will be together
With all those who received your salvation,
And we will be given a crown from You,
For we will be Your pure nation.

We thank You that You redeemed us
And we know that You will come soon
And those who have Your forgiveness,
Are transformed into Your likeness.

You will come as a Judge
For a world that did not want You as its Redeemer,
But for Your children, as a Savior,
Full of mercy and love.

You will bring with You the reward
For our deeds according to Your word,
And You will pronounce judgment
With firmness and righteousness.

April 23, 2009

THE SOWER AND THE SEED

Matthew 13:3-23

One day, the sower left his house
To scatter the seed on the ground
And to bless the place with his word.

The seed fell on different soils,
But it did not sprout everywhere,
And thus from many places
The sower did not reap what he desired.

As for the seeds that fell on hard soil,
When they had to sprout
They were covered by the weeds,
Choked and crushed.

The seeds that fell on rocky places,
Having shallow, undeveloped roots,
Sprouted quickly,
But they withered at the heat of sun.

As for those that fell among thorn bushes,
When they came up
They were covered by the thorns,
And thus they died.

But as for those that fell on good soil
And laid deep roots,
Even if the sun shines
Their fruit grows plentifully.

The one who scattered the seed, the sower,
Is the Lord Jesus, the Savior,
And the seed that fell the ground
Is His precious Word in the Holy scriptures found.

The soil is our souls
Which have to be worked
And thus, little by little,
Are made ready and are transformed.

He who receives the good news
And does not understand its essence
Plants in himself
Much lack of prudence.

Those who received the Word onto stony places are the same
People who heard the Word immediately,
But when trials and serious persecution came
They backed off and got scared quickly.

Those who received the Word among the thorns
Are those who heard the Word,
But the worries of life and the deceit of wealth
Choked it, and deprived the ground of its fruit.

However, those who received the Word on good soil
Are those who hear and understand it,
Choose His promises,
Put them in their souls and are redeemed.

They produce much fruit,
And with humility they bring it to the cross;
With gratitude they sacrifice to You, taking a loss,
And through their lives, they glorify You.

The one who sows with tears
Will reap with joy
And, with the Lord's power and in holy fear,
Will save many souls.

April 26, 2009

REDEEMED

I came to You and You saved me,
You protected me and You redeemed me,
You gave me forgiveness and reconciliation;
And You brought me restoration.

I understand that Your love
Is the greatest treasure;
It can change my nature,
Leading me to Your kingdom above.

Your sacrifice on the cross
Is the gift that brings me
The assurance of eternal life,
And that's why I prostrate myself before Thee.

You ask of me to have faith
And You ask my entire will
That You may change it and work on it
So that its transformation will prove it.

Redeemed from sin –
Oh, what a wonderful thought!
Set aside and made clean,
Through Your sacrifice, we are bought.

Our salvation and redemption are not to our merit,
But You offer them to us as a gift
When in You we believe
And when our eyes to You we lift.

Faith does not come from us,
But is the gift of the Holy Spirit
Which You left on earth;
Help us to not retreat.

Help us not to forget
That we receive of Your grace
Each day that we live,
And thus all the more aware of this we should be.

You called us to take our measures
Of Your divine treasures
And the suffering that You bore in Your body
When You showed Your love to everybody.

Oh, forgive us, Jesus, when many times
We forget about You and show indifference
And total lack of prudence
When we walk through the trials of life.

Salvation, redemption, and peace can come
Only from God, the Father, who
Sent His Son through His great power
And gave us the Holy Spirit when time was due.

May 1, 2009

A Word

Among the multitude of words and actions
I am seeking and waiting for a word –
A word of tenderness and compassion,
A word addressed to me:

A true word,
Clothed with grace;
A word that revives
My being with its strength;

A joyful word,
A lively word,
A good and soothing word,
Full of mercy and power;

A meaningful word,
Valuable and precious,
Sincere and gracious;
A holy and powerful word.

I want your word to be spoken with sincerity,
With understanding and meekness;
An edifying word full of purity
And carrying a message of kindness.

But when I talk with people,
Many of them do not know the truth,
But among themselves they advise each other,
And thus they use words for all evil and for many to bother.

A word said in season
Is like a honeycomb,
And thus the soul needs not fear
Because the word is calm and clear.

Through words one can be justified
And also through words one can be accused,
But only through the Word of God
Can one be holy and glorified.

Through a word one can build up
Or one can destroy;
One can strengthen someone,
And also with a word one can pray.

I came to you to hear a word,
With my heart wanting
To be able to see the good in you
And to look into your soul.

A word says much;
It describes who you and who you touch
By whether or not you encourage others
In the commotion of their struggles.

So, pay attention to how you speak
And to which words you pick;
Be careful what you tell
To the human soul.

A good word spoken to one in pain
Is to the soul and body a gain
When it is pronounced with sensitivity
And applied with generosity.

A word that warms the soul
Is a word of blessing –
A word of thanksgiving,
Coming from your thoughts.

A thoughtful word and a tested word
Is a word that is carried in the soul,
That protects and loves,
And that speaks of You, Lord.

Many times words are used
For condemnation and for judgment,
And thus many were hurt by them
And fell into discouragement.

Also through words
Legalism was perpetuated,
And thus the soul was destroyed
And enslaved by it.

So long as you are on this earth,
Use only the Word of God,
For in it you can trust,
And by it you can last.

May 1, 2009

Our Refuge and Strength

Psalm 46:1-3

The Lord "is our refuge and strength,
A very present help in trouble" –
A help that comes to us, wherever we are,
And helps us to depart from the vanities of life.

When trials came – large or small –
We could stand strong in You,
For You called us to Yourself, and thus we all
Were saved and made new.

When fear tried to come again,
Making us live in pain,
It made us feel our guilt,
And much trouble it built.

It made us think
Only of the trial we were going through
And made us see
How our great dilemma grew:

The dilemma that despite Your power,
We still see that our nature
Is weak, corrupted, and fearful.
But it can become thankful.

In our battle against fear and powerlessness,
You sent us, through our faith, the realization
That You gave us a spirit of power and meditation
That heals our pain and cleanses us of our wickedness.

So, You remind us that when trials come,
You are our refuge and tower,
And even if the mountains shake with great power,
They will not frighten us.

I need Your prudence,
And to not trust in my experience,
Which makes me believe only in what I know
And totally forget Your work here below.

May 13, 2009

The Train of Life

I boarded the train of life when I was born,
And quickly I traveled through life, arriving
At different destinations, where I could see
Many people getting off.

The train went through mountains and valleys,
And I could see good people as well as those who were bad –
Those with pure souls and thoughts, by You led,
And those who got entangled in their ways.

On the train I could see untold beauty
Everywhere, even on the tops of the mountains;
And in the depths of the valleys low
I did not see anything that was without purpose there below

Valley with grass and with flowers,
With a pleasant and relaxing smell,
All your beauty and all your wonder
Want your story to tell.

We arrived at the station called Patience
Where I had to remain for a long time;
Where compassion was shown to me
And I learned how to live.

And this very train
Made a stop at the station called Relationship,
Where many of us have desired to arrive
In order to build life's foundation.

From here, still farther,
The train went up quickly along winding paths,
And it stopped at the station called Friendships,
Where I met much hypocrisy in relationships.

The train bypassed many places
And it arrived at the station called Love,
Where a great story started,
And where people rested.

But many were not ready
To take the responsibility
That love brings
Or to walk on the path where it leads.

From here we headed for the station called Pleasure,
Where we arrived with much silence,
And after a time spent in it,
We felt its pain in full measure.

Then we arrived at the station called Lust,
Where we stopped with eager desire,
And without realization we were caught in its fire,
Entering into the world of the dreams from our past;

And then the train went farther
And I saw many separating roads, and passing by,
There was the road of Hatred and the road of Lie,
As well as the road of Truth and that of Wonder.

From here we arrived at the station called Faith,
And from there we went towards Victory;
But on the way, I stumbled and I fell,
And then was when I saw You and when You made me well.

I saw You when You helped me,
When You carried me in Your arms,
When You reminded me that You love me
And that on the journey You keep me from sin's attacks.

From the station of Faith,
We stopped at the station named Marriage,
Where this journey reached the place
Where my strength was proven and pledged:

Strength in thought and in love,
Strength in total giving,
Strength in faith and living,
And strength in will, through power from above.

Here, in marriage, I experienced companionship,
And I received my children as a gift;
Here I also had to learn true friendship,
And I needed many prayers toward You to lift.

In this union
I experienced feelings of both sadness and joy,
And I had a great longing
To be closer to You, Jesus.

And then we stopped at the station called Family,
Where I have spent most of my time on earth;
The place where I learned with joy
To apply Your Word.

In the end we all got onto the train,
Together with the children,
And thus they felt life's terrain,
Preparing them for the storms of life that would gather.

Passing through the city of Joy,
We all looked around,
And in it we could enjoy
All the blessings that here abound.

And then we stopped at the station called Righteousness,
Which comes from the Lord Jesus
When our souls and spirits are obedient
And filled with His great love.

And now we are still on the train,
Traveling towards the final destination,
And we desire Your protection
Over our entire lives so that we will not run in vain.

For we desire to arrive at the place promised by You –
The place that we cannot imagine even in our dreams –
To hear spoken to us, "good and faithful servant,"
At the place where we will see You, Jesus Christ.

Finally, the last destination
Is the station named Eternity,
Where there is no limitation
And where we want to arrive with joy and purity.

Are you ready – am I ready –
To stand before Jesus?
The price was paid at Golgotha with great love
So that we can enter in the heavens above.

If you do not know Him now
Oh, come, sinful soul, before Him bow;
Come to Jesus Christ,
Come and start your walk with Him.

May 17, 2009

My Friend is the One Who...

My friend is the one who
Through the storms of life stands strong
And does not allow himself to be defeated due
To the wounds that his sufferings prolong.

My friend is the one who cries
And who humbles his heart
To be a help and a blessing
To an eternal soul that is seeking.

My friend is the one who encourages others,
Lifts them up, and emboldens them;
The one who knows to give an honest embrace;
The one who knows to be modest and shows others grace.

My friend is the one who knows how to listen,
And does not desire many words;
The one who is patient,
The one who is self-giving and looks to You, Lord.

My friend is the one who is misunderstood,
The one who in life chose
To walk on a path that is clean and straight
And sprinkled with drops of mercy.

My friend is the one who looks above
And chooses as his Savior Jesus Christ,
For then we have a common base,
Knowing that we will receive the crown of life, in His love.

My friend is the one who visits
Orphans, the poor, and those with illnesses of all kinds,
Thus using the model
Of the Bible, which encourages us.

My friend is the one who truly loves,
And who through wisdom is strengthened,
Sacrificing his comfort
To show to the afflicted support.

My friend is the one who knows how to thank,
The one who knows to speak well –
With essence and power –
Thus healing many of their pain.

My friend is the one who knows how to communicate
And who understands unique situations
Of listening and helping,
The one who knows to show his input.

My friend is the one who suffers and is mistreated,
The one who united his life with Jesus and in Him believed,
The one who cries in pain to God
To help him to temper his ego through Jesus' blood.

My friend is the one who stands for a principle
Though he is isolated, left alone,
And surrounded by hatred;
For he remains determined in his soul.

May 19, 2009

SALVATION

In Your great love
You gave us Your salvation –
Salvation of our souls which are burdened
With sin and pressed by pain.

Help us through Your love
To grow in the knowledge of You,
And help us not to forget
That You have made us new.

Salvation was given to us as a gift
Through Your great grace –
Without money or payment from us –
Allowing us to see Your face.

Our salvation cost You
When You gave Your Son on the cross;
He carried our sins upon His body, and took a great loss
And thus He guaranteed to us eternal life.

Salvation opened for us the door to eternity
Spent with Jesus forever,
The proof of His kindness
Shown to you and me ever.

In exchange for such a great gift,
We bring to You our nothingness,
And we wish, through our conduct,
To be obedient to You and to put on Your meekness.

I do not have anything else to bring to You,
And I do not have enough words to thank You,
But towards You my steps lead
As I wish to serve You with my life and creed.

You called us to come to You
And put aside ourselves,
To put on repentance
Along with love and faith.

You set us apart and You took our strife
And You wrote our names in the Book of Life;
Thus You sealed us with Your name
When You called us to Yourself and find in us no blame.

Salvation – oh, what a wonderful word –
Exists always in our souls.
It soothed our pain
And gave us great gain.

Salvation brought us the responsibility
To tell others about Your kindness,
To live with joy, hope, humility,
Balance and confidence.

Salvation, you changed my thinking
And gave me a new way of speaking;
Thus I humbly dare
To bring to You, Lord, the burdens I bear.

Through Your salvation, You
Changed my gaze,
My wishes, and my longings, giving me in life a new phase,
Helping me look to You and making me new.

Salvation comes through Golgotha,
From Your cross,
From Your torn body
And from Your holy blood shed for everybody.

Your salvation comes through renunciation;
It comes through Your great power;
It comes from the road that leads
To the place where Your cross is.

Salvation comes when in life you are
At the limit of your strength,
For then is when you desire
To walk upon Jesus' path for the rest of its length.

May 27, 2009

BE ATTENTIVE!

In the morning when you wake up, be
Attentive to what you see;
Be attentive to any sound
That is around.

Listen quietly to the songs of the birds
And look at them with joy.
Look at the animals that desire
To live; take heed of them, and admire.

Then, look at the sun so bright –
Giver of life and light,
Which warms us with its heat
And helps us our sadness to defeat.

And do not forget to be attentive to the flowers
Of many shapes and colors,
And to the green, beautiful grass;
And do not doubt, but believe.

Believe that all that you see and hear
Is the masterpiece of the great Creator,
And thus with humility come and praise
The Wonderful Master, and His name raise

Jesus Christ is His name,
The most beautiful name of all, without any blame
And like none other on earth below;
A name worthy to proclaim.

He also created the clouds of the expanse of heaven
And made them to gather in the sky;
And upon them His authority He laid,
Ordering them to satisfy the earth with rain.

He created the cool rain of the morning
Which refreshes our lives,
And formed the white snow, which falls
As proof of His power and love.

And be attentive to the tall mountains –
To their incomparable majesty –
And remember that He created them also.

Take time to see and to hear the spring that runs smoothly,
Stop and look at it fully;
It's as if it speaks to you with words sublime
About a sweet and beautiful time.

And in the evening, watch with attention
The stars and the moon, which give us inspiration
With their light, accompanying us
Along the motion of the earth.

And look at the ant;
Look at how small it is, and how
Without having a ruler or commander
It prepares its food in the summer.

In the harvest time it gathers its food
And helps its companions
To live and to multiply for the colony's good,
Thus fulfilling its role.

And for everything, learn to be thankful;
Live your life and be careful.
For it goes by quickly, with great speed,
And takes us with it.

It takes us to the end of our existence on this earth
In the presence of the Holy Lord,
And we will stand before His royal throne
If we have received Him and have had the second birth.

And look at yourself, the most wonderful creation –
The most complex and the most advanced,
And do not forget, that you are under His protection,
And that He carries you in His arms.

So, do not abuse what He has given you;
Be attentive, keep it pure –
The gift and the talent invested in you –
Use it for His glory, and be blessed.

June 2, 2009

LORD, YOUR WORDS

Lord, may Your words
Be real in my heart;
And help me, through them, to do my part.

Help me to be taken neither by multitudes of words
Nor by all kinds of ideas nor by any fear;
Rather let Your words penetrate me, Lord,
Deep in my soul, and let them be near.

I desire for Your words
To change me, oh, Lord,
Transforming me and then taking me
Through the domain of Your will, that there I might be.

I do not desire to transmit Your words only to other people
And to destine them to change;
Instead I desire for Your lovely call
To resound in my heart and awaken my soul.

Lord, Your words are full of power;
And when I have them within me,
I grow strong, and they make me a follower
Of You and of Your will.

June 5, 2009

THE ARMOR OF GOD

Ephesians 6:14-17

Believing in You, Lord,
I am engaged in a spiritual war
Against an adversary, who with madness
Persecutes Your children and provokes much sadness.

In the life of faith I found out
That I have to be a soldier well armed
With Your divine armor,
Which will bring us full victory in this war.

Our fight is not against the things that we see,
But is a cruel fight against the spirits of darkness
And against the evil of the deep
That we may restore the lost values of godliness.

For we do not have to wrestle against flesh and blood
But against the principalities, and the rulers of darkness,
Against the spiritual wickedness in the heavenly places;
For You, take away our spiritual blindness.

That is why we have to put on
The armor of God:
So that we may remain standing
In the fight that surrounds us.

Having our waist girded with truth
We are able to remove all evil
And wearing the breastplate of righteousness
We are able to spread the fragrance of Your kindness.

With the preparation of the gospel may we shod our feet,
And having the shield of faith to protect us,
We are able to quench all the evil darts.

On our head we should have the helmet of salvation,
For we find ourselves at war with our nature;
But the Word of God brings us His invitation
To have it with us always, and in it to find our pleasure.

We know that in You is victory
Which brings us peace, hope, and joy;
Because You are the One who suffered much,
And with Your sacrifice on the cross, our spirits You touch.

You gave us full victory and showed us Your love
When You resurrected from the dead,
And thus You brought us the truth that led
Us to the reality of the power from above.

June 5-6, 2009

ASSURANCE

In You I have assurance,
Not in my performance,
But in Your great love and salvation,
Which brought me redemption.

The assurance of my forgiven sin
Came when You met me,
When on the path of my life
You came to take away my strife.

In the moment when You granted me forgiveness,
And through Your blood, reconciliation,
You opened the widely the door
In order that I might come to You, just as You foretold.

When I entered through the door, You received me,
Giving me rest and peace;
And I found springs of living water,
Hope, love, joy, and release from my troubles,

There fear and hatred did not touch me,
For in You I was protected;
Light and hope surrounded me,
And liberty in You I obtained.

Your blessed assurance
Is the only hope for us all;
It keeps us strong,
And makes us worthy of Your call.

There is no safer place –
No place better or purer –
Where I feel so blessed
Other than that of being hidden in You.

In You my need is fulfilled
And the thirst of my soul is quenched;
In You, I came to know true life
When I took You as my guide.

June 6, 2009

MERCY, KINDNESS, MEEKNESS

Colossians 3:12-16

Lord, You chose us to stand,
To be holy and loved,
And You led us understand
How much by You we are watched.

You told us to put on mercy and kindness;
Humility, meekness and patience;
To bear each others burdens;
And to forgive the mistakes of many.

But above all we have
To clothe ourselves with love and joy,
Which is the bond of perfection
And the proof of our redemption.

Then the peace of God
Will always dwell in our lives,
Teaching us to thank You, giving us Your light,
And helping us to love as You have loved;

And the Word of God will dwell richly within us,
Teaching us, in all wisdom, to trust,
Showing us how to live bearing Your name,
And reminding us that from of old You are the same.

June 17, 2009

A Beautiful Day

Today You gave us
A beautiful and serene day,
A day with clear blue sky,
A day filled with Your care;

A day in which I saw again
How You have taken care of everyone,
A day in which I could gain
Encouragement for my soul from You, the Holy One.

I looked at the green grass and the beautiful flowers
With their petals of different colors,
Wanting to be able to express their mystery
Through the power of words.

I saw how perfectly You created them
And how You gave them beauty
With colors and different forms,
As they are kept by Your love and authority.

The beautiful red roses
Remind us that we ought to be serious
In starting our days with You, even in our losses,
And to trust in You, who are so precious.

They remind us of Your blood,
Shed for us sinners and given in full,
Gathering together all of us who trod
The path that leads to You and makes us joyful.

The yellow flowers remind us
Of the rays of sunlight that warm us,
While those pink, blue, and violet, through Your grace,
Put smiles on our faces.

The white flowers tell us about purity
And remind us of our responsibility
To remain in Your righteousness,
Devoted to Your cause in its fullness.

But in my life I had a day
Even more beautiful than this:
The day when the evidence of Yourself
Brought me to You, Jesus, and taught me to obey.

This was the day when You met me
In my foolish running,
The day when You saved me
And brought to an end my searching.

This was the most beautiful day –
When You took my sins away,
When I was from the darkness snatched,
And when by You my spirit was touched.

Yet another beautiful day
Is the day when I have another chance
To look to You for You my soul to cleanse
And my sin to forgive, which before You I lay.

But the most beautiful day will be
The day when we will see You face-to-face,
When we will be clothed in immortality
Through You great love and grace.

June 17, 2009

WE ARE WAITING EAGERLY FOR YOU, JESUS

With our hearts and our eyes directed up above,
We look to the heavens and we are waiting for You to come
That we may be with You and that You may take us home
To see Your face and Your glory, as proof of Your love.

The hour is late and the darkness is deep
And within myself, I cry,
For the fear and dread of the night presses me,
And yet, my heart does not leave You, and You stand by.

In the night watch, when all is quiet,
I call to You through sobs, for I am Your beloved child;
And I ask You to be with me, to protect me,
For I know that You love me and that You want me to be free.

Many times when great storms arise
I run to You with confidence and longing,
And with my eyes on the prize,
Because to You I belong.

In the night of this life
The path becomes all the narrower,
And walking upon it
Your presence becomes sweeter:

For then is when I adore You
And when I eagerly wait for You
To come with Your light
And to make my life new.

I wait for You to come with Your justice and love,
And thus to bring to us Your redemption;
For You to banish all that is old, to bring us renewal from above,
And to help us to remain in Your will, desiring Your salvation.

Everything is subject to You
And bows before You;
And may everyone who has breath come to You in humility,
For You have put in their souls the thought of eternity.

From where I was, away from Your sight,
You took me and gave me Your salvation;
You gave me Your light
Along with divine revelation.

June 18, 2009

THE CHURCH

You have put us in the church
And You have told us not to be afraid of anything,
But to fear only You,
Since this leads to wisdom.

You have told us that we are the church,
That in us You will dwell,
That we must serve You with our life and our song,
And that Your mystery to us You will explain.

You have told us that the Holy Spirit will help us
To feel Your presence
And to learn mercy and perseverance,
Goodness and forgiveness.

You have told us to buy pure gold
From You, our King;
To drink clean water,
Blessed by You; and to become wiser.

You have also told us that in the church
You ought to be above all
That is seen and heard,
And that You are to be feared.

Your church has passed and still passes
Through a time of cold persecution –
Through a time of pain and suffering –
When her faith and determination are tested.

Today the church is attacked
And as always, is targeted;
In many places Christians scatter;
They doubt Your love, and falter.

Many do not remain steadfast – neither on the way,
Nor upon Your promises,
And they try to take on another form,
Forgetting to obey.

Thus, many places of worship
Are almost empty and fail to resound;
The ugliness of the world
Makes present its sound;

And there is no difference
Between Your people and the world,
And in this way Your name and Your Word
In the world have no defense.

The church is in need of repentance,
Humility, and faith, so that by Your might
It may again be able to be salt and light
In a world full of pretense.

Your sacrifice still has power
To renew and transform,
To give blessing,
And to bring to life reform.

June 18, 2009

Oh, Lord, When I Gaze at You

Oh, Lord, when I gaze at You
My heart is filled with joy,
And then is when I desire
My thoughts to employ.

When I look at the world, created
Through Your holy Word,
I can see Your wonderful power
Acting upon this earth.

When I see all the creatures that adorn nature,
How they look to You for help,
My soul desires to rejoice
As I feel so much Your love;

And when I see that all You have done
Exists for a purpose –
How You gave everything a time to begin,
A time of growth and of receiving Your love in abundance –

Then, I thank You
And I glorify You,
For You are my Sustainer,
And my life's Protector;

And when the time comes
For me to head towards heavenly glory,
Your protective arms
Will help me to have wisdom and victory.

Help me to joyfully wait, Lord,
To see Your greatness;
And then to hear Your just Word
Welcoming me into Your kingdom's brightness.

Your Word that is just and yet loving,
That is powerful and life-giving,
Will impart to us our reward
And will remind us of the payment for our sin.

July 11, 2009

WITH MY GAZE FIXED

With our gaze fixed on You, we start to walk,
And with You we want to be
That we may have Your guidance,
Sense Your love, and be free.

With my gaze fixed on You, the waters will not overwhelm me
When they want to pass over me;
Neither will the fire cause harm,
For I am protected by Your strong arm.

For You are my God,
And I am Your child,
And because I am loved,
You proclaim to me Your power.

You are the Holy One of Israel,
God, the great Savior,
Who with Your powerful arm brings us through trials,
Protecting us, divine Lamb.

With my gaze fixed on You, I can walk on water
Without doubt, without fear;
For when I am looking at You, You ask me to come near;
Then with assurance I bow before You.

But when my eyes are on the waves,
I am subject to many attacks
Of lack of assurance and lack of strength,
Of lack of confidence and lack of faith.

The aim of my life is You, Jesus:
An aim that carries me upward;
It is my great reward,
Which revives and strengths my life.

July 12, 2009

PRAYER

Lord, I thank You for the gift of prayer
Which breaks the power of fear,
A gift which You want to manifest in my life
As I take You as my guide.

Through prayer I can come to You just as I am
Because You have promised that You receive me;
Tenderly, You tell me that You love me, divine Lamb;
You want to make me holy and to help me see.

In prayer we come to You with thanksgiving,
Praises, reverence, and singing;
And through Your power I direct my gaze
Towards Your great grace.

In prayer we mediate for others,
And with sincerity wish
That they also come to love You
And thus be made entirely new.

In prayer we bring before You
The authorities who rule over us,
And we ask You to make them not forget
That they owe You their lives.

In prayer we bring to You those who are sick,
As well as those who think of themselves as being brave,
And we ask You to heal the former
But to humble the latter.

Through true prayer
We learn humility,
We learn the true union
Of love and piety.

Prayer is the manner through which I come to You
With my soul heavy and full
Of fears, pains, joys and victories;
I come to You perseveringly.

In prayer I ask the Holy Spirit
To come and to help me with His Word,
That thus all evil may disappear
And Your Holy presence appear,

To overwhelm and to bless me,
And with Your Holy Spirit to baptize me,
That, having in You my spiritual food,
I may have as my life's purpose to apply Your good.

July 17, 2009

BLESSING

Oh, what a blessing to my life it has been,
Jesus, since I found You,
Since You snatched me from the world of sin.

What a great blessing it is,
With each day that passes,
Even in the cold mornings,
To see how Your story is unfolding.

The greatest blessing
Is Your salvation,
Paid with a price that
Proved Your love and passion:

A price with no comparison,
A price of blood shed for everybody,
A price paid with Your holy body
To free us from our soul's prison.

What a blessing to be able to look
At everything that You have created through Your power,
That through all You have made You may be glorified
And in our lives magnified.

Trials are a blessing,
Although passing through them is hard;
For by them You bring us from afar
That we may seek You and learn thanksgiving.

Through trials You teach us patience,
And You show us that we are nothing –
Without You, our little souls lack their radiance;
Away from You, they wither.

Through trials You bring us closer to Yourself,
And You help us to trust
That only You can make everything new
When with Your love You surround us.

You have told us that all works
For the good of all who love You,
For the good of those few
Who feel Your presence close.

Another blessing is our mind,
Which You gave us to use for Your glory;
Having within us Your story
We keep our souls rooted in You.

The health that You give us
Shows us Your mercy
For us, mere sinners,
With souls which for You are thirsty.

Health is a great blessing
Which we bring to You with reverence
That, in using it for You,
It may bring us much benefit.

July 28, 2009

You Showed Me

When You met me,
You showed me
The state of my sin
And where I had been.

You showed me the price of my redemption –
A price sealed with blood –
Which brought me Your salvation,
Cleansed me, and showed me Your love.

You showed me how, on the path of life,
Many times I lost You from my sight,
And how wandering around in my strife
I forgot entirely of Your might.

You showed me how I believed in myself
Without remembering You,
How for a while I believed in chance and luck and self,
Thus being entangled in the maze of life.

You showed me my deceitful heart,
Which many times deluded me,
Making me from You to depart
And separating me from You, leaving me lonely.

You showed me the means through which
I can receive Your blessing:
Looking up to You,
The Lord of life, Jesus.

You showed me that I can come to You
Each time I feel tired and without hope,
For You will receive me
And You make me new.

You showed how You stand by me,
Helping me to mature and to grow,
And how through trials and tribulations I can see
You opening the treasures of Your love here below.

Jesus, You showed me the cross
Which stands lifted up even today,
And how upon it, through Your loss,
My burden was taken away.

You showed me the patience with which
You work in my life,
And how with Your blessing
You encourage me in my fight.

You showed me the gift of suffering,
Which cannot be neglected;
For through it, my life was corrected
And You carried me to the peak of victory.

You showed me that only with humility
And with a contrite heart
Can I obtain true joy and purity,
Through Your sacrificed life.

You showed me Your faithfulness,
Which many times, with tenderness,
Reminds me of You
And does to me only good.

You showed me that each time I make a mistake
And fall while on Your path,
Your strong arms, for Your name's sake,
Surround me and strengthen my walk.

You showed me how You carry me in Your arms
And how You take me from the depths of pain,
And thus I felt Your great love, my richest gain,
While advancing all the more upon the path of life.

You showed me how You can use
My limitations, my nothingness, my experiences
Through Your grace we may arrive....
Where it will be seen that nothing was wasted.

You showed me that only through You can I stand;
And that some day I will see Your face
Because my name is in the Book of Life from beforehand,
Just as You have foretold from the very beginning in Your grace.

You showed me Your Holy Spirit
As it is described in Your Word, whose power has no limit;
A Spirit full of strength and peace,
Before Whom my words cease.

Considering all that You showed me
My soul was left overwhelmed,
Seeing how You unfolded Your plan
Because You loved me.

And now I come to thank You
For a faith as a seed of mustard,
And to tell You how much I desire
To put all upon the altar.

May You help me to live
According to Your plan
And to proclaim Your salvation,
Helping those with guilty souls to believe.

August 8, 2009

THE RIGHTEOUS ONE

Psalm 1:1-6

You have brought us onto the path of righteousness
And You have paid for our sin with the gift of love,
Which took You on the path of pain and loneliness
And took from us the weight of our burdens.

The righteous one does not stand in the path of sinners,
Nor does he sit in the seat of the scornful;
For he associates himself with Your children,
With the loving and humble.

His delight is in the law of the Lord
And he lives by the power of the Word;
He meditates on it day and night
And he directs his gaze to the Lord and His might.

The righteous one is like a tree
Planted by a river of water for the reason
Of bringing forth its fruit in the proper season.

Its leaves do not wither,
And whatever he does he brings to a good end;
Thus the leaves get stronger,
Showing us how much You want to become our friend.

The ungodly are like chaff which the wind drives away
And scatters across the earth;
They will not be able to stand on the judgment day,
Because they do not have the spiritual birth.

For the Lord knows the way of the righteous
Because they are fed and protected by Him,
But the way of the unrighteous
Leads to the destruction of the deceivers.

August 31, 2009

MY REDEMPTION

Isaiah 12:1-6

I praise You, Lord, that though You were angry with me,
Your anger turned away and You comforted me,
Calling me to You,
Offering to make me completely new.

The Lord is my salvation
And I will be full of faith;
He gives me redemption
And forgives my past.

He has told me not to fear anything
And to continue to look to Him,
But I come, Lord, to confess to You and to bring
My soul which, in storms, becomes dim.

You are the reason for my praises
And the strength in which I stand,
Who with power rescues me out of slavery;
Before You my knee I bend.

I praise You that You had mercy on me
And that You saved my soul;
You asked me my heart, my life, my all,
Showing me how to be free.

With joy we will draw water from the wells of salvation
And we will taste from the depths of love;
With Your help we will stand
Victoriously before You.

Let us praise and proclaim His name,
And with power let us transmit it to others;
Let us remember His greatness,
Our life's richness.

Let us sing His name and keep His Word –
For He has done marvelous things –
Let us exalt the precious name of the Lord
And His beloved deeds.

May all His works
Be made known over all the earth
So that it may be clear that due to His grace
They can be seen.

Let us rejoice and be glad,
For He is our shelter;
And through Jesus may we become stronger,
Remembering how for us He bled.

August 31, 2009

I Know

Walking on the path of life,
Even at the dawn of the day,
I feel You close to me,
And I know that I am with You on my way.

I know that Your Spirit lives within me, that my mind He clears,
And that He guides me with love in this world;
He helps me just as You have told,
And in prayer, with me, He perseveres.

He shows me my heart just as it is
And how I can become holy;
He directs me towards Jesus Christ –
Towards the spring of love that flows so beautifully.

I know I did not deserve Your love,
For I angered You much,
And while on far and foreign paths, I felt Your touch
Which brought me to You and lifted me above.

You took my life – wounded
And broken in pieces –
A life interrupted by pain
And full of great burdens:

A shattered life,
Full of strife;
A life divided,
Yet received by You.

I know that only You were able
To make from such a life
A work so great
That it would be unbelievable.

I know that only You give me direction
And that only You can make in me correction
To bring fulfillment and sensitivity,
Reflection and sensibility.

May You give me an abundant life
That is devoted to You,
That in Your might
I may make a difference for the better.

I also know that in this new life
I need You as a guide
To bless me and to strengthen me
And to walk with me upon the path.

For without You life has no meaning
And thus we cannot understand it;
Without You the life is dry
And all our days are a continuous cry.

I know that our new life
Cost You dearly
Because You loved us and took our fight,
And thus our thanksgiving rises from our souls.

I know that You gave us eternal life
When we let You
Penetrate to the depths of our hearts
With Your Holy Trinity and Your truth.

May You bring us healing
And reconciliation with Yourself;
May You give us Your joy
And take away our pride.

May You help us to be useful to others
That we may not live in vain,
For thus we may give our new lives
For You according to Your plan.

September 6, 2009

FOR YOUR WEDDING

At last the day has come
Which by you has been long awaited,
When with emotion and love you will give your whole lives
To each other and thus have your burdens lifted.

This is the most beautiful day
Which in your hearts and minds will leave
Unforgettable memories
That you will carry in your souls' treasuries.

Marriage is a sacred covenant
Instituted by the Lord for our contentment,
A covenant made for life
If you will take Him as your guide.

I wish that the Lord Jesus will be the center
Of your bond of love both now and later
So that on the road of life, daily,
You will see His guidance plainly.

If you live according to the principles of Scripture
You will experience the depths of love –
Pure and sacrificial love that is a picture
Of Him who came from above.

You, man, are called to love as Christ
Loved the church and gave Himself for her
To clean and to sanctify the sinner,
To strengthen him and thus transform his life.

And you, wife, in this love,
Are called to respond
And with respect to penetrate
Into the thinking of your husband.

May you be one in heart and mind
Just as He has told us to,
Thus together you will find
That you two can have humble hearts.

May you be open with each other
And make communication a common practice,
For thus all your life will be blessed
And your bond will be intense.

Do not forget prayer,
Which is the greatest power
That in the storms of life will bring calm,
Strengthening your bond with its balm.

The reading of the Word together
Will form the crown of life,
And when trials and tribulations gather
It will free you from the peak of pain.

May you learn to lean on Him
For the life that you build together as a team,
For thus your offspring will understand
What the bond is that ties you together, helping you to stand.

Thus you will be blessed
And helped by the Messiah and His Word,
And your life will have a purpose upon this earth:
Showing others the power of the Holy Lord.

September 8, 2009

The Bond of Love and Peace

You have asked us to conduct ourselves in a manner worthy
Of the calling that You have given us,
And with strength and faith
To make You known to others.

You have told us to walk through life with radiance;
With humility, meekness, and with much patience;
And from the treasures of love to take
Our life's song,

In Your love You have told us to preserve
The unity of the Spirit and the bond of peace
As You teach us in Your Scripture;
May You help us our hearts for You to reserve.

For there is only one God,
The Father of everyone, above all,
Who works amazingly in all
And Who saves us from hardship.

There is only one Lord, one God,
One faith, one baptism;
And I work at knowing You better in my soul
With Your help, as I give You my all.

September 13, 2009

I Wanted to Speak with You

I wanted to speak with you
And to give you my heart,
But you stayed far away from me
And left me apart.

I wanted to tell you so many things
Which could have brought so much good,
I wanted to tell you how my life to yours clings
And that I wish to be with you.

I wanted to tell you that when you look
At me with warmth and love,
It delights my whole being,
And it cheers me up.

I wanted to tell you how God
Changed my life and brought me His redemption,
And how my soul, by Him loved,
Found its salvation.

I wanted to tell you how healing
Was offered to me as a gift,
And how my thinking
Was transformed through grace and was redeemed.

I wanted to tell you more about the way,
About how I came to know forgiveness and love,
And about how I came to obey
Jesus, who gave me salvation from above.

I wanted to share with you my thinking
And to make known to you my feelings;
I wanted to hear your whisper,
To feel your love, and to know that you care.

I wanted for you to open your heart to me,
To hold me to close your heart,
To keep me as near to yourself as you can;
And I wanted to be able to feel you as one with me.

Thoughts, dreams, struggles I wanted then to share,
To be one in feelings and actions
And to live with passion
Our love and our union.

I wanted to feel your protection
And to be able to offer you the beauty
Of a pure and devoted soul
Presented to you in whole.

But you did not want to communicate,
Through silence and indifference you isolated me,
And thus a great wall between us was built.

You did not want to come close to me,
To love me as you should,
Thus to work together to do good,
Knowing that is how we should be.

Again I felt alone,
Surrounded by the adversities of life,
Alone before the difficulties and prone
To the pressure of pain and strife.

Then in my distress
I invoked the power of God,
And thus my life by Him was touched,
For towards Him I press.

Only He can bring you healing,
Give you strength,
Put joy in your soul, and bring
His great love in all its breadth and length.

September 15, 2009

No Other God

I must always remind myself that by You I am loved,
And that there is no other God
Than You – Jehovah, the Creator,
Messiah, our Savior.

You – Who created all that is seen
And Whose voice all nature obeys –
You are the One who says
That I should depart from evil and not take it in.

You are my only help
When trials come and make me weak;
You are my sole Protector
When the heavy waves hit me.

You are the One Who responds to our prayers
And You penetrate us with Your love;
You carry us in Your strong arms
And give us eternal blessings.

You are the One Who came to earth
And took upon the cross our curse,
The One who brought to us God's Word
And the Holy Spirit as a sword.

In great joys and pleasures
You are the One Who looks on us,
And in moments of silence You open to us Your treasures
And tell us that in You we should trust.

When in the beauty of life
Temptations of all kinds come,
In You we find stability at the dawn of the day,
And thus many pains are kept away.

You are the One Who cares for us,
The One Who gives us all that we need,
And through Your Holy Spirit,
You show us Your will.

All nature listens to You,
All that is seen and all that is not seen responds to You,
And the power of Your profound Word
Disarms any insult.

You are the only One Who came to us
And freed us from the burden of sin;
You are the One Who granted us forgiveness,
And thus in You we found liberty.

You are the One Who brought us healing
And the One Who changed our nature,
Replacing with Your love the hatred
Which separates us from You.

You are the only One Who has guaranteed our eternity –
And a sublime place for us You have prepared –
The One who took our burdens, because You cared,
When we came to You in humility.

No one can compare with You,
The One Who put in our souls hope that is true,
The One Who put us face-to-face with who we are
And made our souls and minds subject to Your love.

October 2, 2009

Autumn

Autumn came with its beauty as from of old,
With many colors and with wonderful mornings,
Though sometimes bringing rain and cold,
Making us suffer.

Colors of all kinds
Combine so beautifully;
Seeing them soothes our minds
And delights us fully.

The leaves of the trees form such a stunning landscape;
They create a wonderful collage;
And every one of them shows us
The care that You have for us.

Every leaf has its own place
And its own time to live,
And then it changes its color
At Your instruction.

After a certain length of time,
The colored leaf is taken by the wind
And thus separates itself from its world
At the moment it is so told.

So it happens with each leaf,
And after a time, the tree is bare,
And it prepares itself for the cruel winter,
Which comes like a thief.

Oh, Lord, I thank you for all the seasons –
For their diversity, wonder, and beauty –
Because through them I see how You have a reason,
And how You are always present.

I see how the animals look to You
For help and for food,
And how You heal any wound
Of the people who love You.

You likewise prepare us for the winter of life,
So that, with You, we can face it
As we seek Your presence, Your might,
And the guidance of Your Holy Spirit.

Thus passing through winter,
When the ground is cold and frozen
And as I leave others behind crying,
I am saved by You; I know where I am going.

Saved and received by You on high
To spend eternity with You, Jesus,
Is a special grace, a grace divine,
A privilege that I do not deserve and yet is mine.

Your grace is an unmerited mercy
Given to us who have received You;
And our desperate souls,
In You, were found.

I will have untold joy in You;
My soul will rejoice in You;
For You have clothed me with the garment of salvation,
You have given me Your righteousness and Your redemption.

October 21, 2009

TIME

You have given us time to prepare ourselves
And to come to You with everything,
To prostrate ourselves before You
And to not forget about You.

Time is the greatest gift,
Given to us in grace
That it may be useful
In our living for Christ.

A time was ordered by You –
A particular season –
To be used for the reason
Of producing fruit and becoming new.

Time was created by You
And You have put limitations on it.
At the proper time You showed us Your love;
You gave us Jesus, Your Son.

At the appointed time
You came to earth
And brought us forgiveness
Through Your great sacrifice.

Many times, time is used manipulatively;
Often it is misused intentionally –
For personal gain it is exploited;
And frequently it is unappreciated.

Time is occupied by many things;
It is filled with many concerns.
In this way it passes quickly and it goes by;
And thus we carry our crosses.

Time can bring us healing
And God's blessing
If we come to Jesus in humility
And receive His love in all its purity.

Time can also bring us pain
When we use it in only for our own gain.
Therefore, be wise and choose
The law of His love.

Make a good and healthy decision
So that you may be able to maintain a joyful heart
And so that your life may be fulfilled,
Having a purpose and a direction.

October 29, 2009

Your Heart

You have told us to preserve our hearts
With care and prudence,
Because from the heart flow the springs of life
Which can melt the coldness of indifference.

From the abundance of the heart, the mouth speaks
And from it we love or hate, as You have told.
From it we suffer and from it we sympathize,
And when we are negligent, our hearts become cold.

From it come evil things,
Corrupt thoughts and actions,
And pain that troubles us
To the point of overcoming us.

Our hearts must be changed
And raised up to You,
And our selves subjected
To You, the Lord of life, Jesus.

Pride is the enemy of the heart
Which holds it far from You
And takes us to the depths of the pit; it is the start
Of the evil that follows after it soon.

That is why You want from us a broken heart
And a contrite spirit which desires You:
So that we can be set apart
And be made entirely new.

So, take care of your heart that you may have no regrets;
Take care and do not forget
That only in Jesus can you find
The peace, love, and hope that you desire.

October 29, 2009

The Rain and Your Care

Today when I got up
And when the phone rang,
I had to ready myself quickly
And get on the road.

There was still a deep darkness,
And looking outside I saw
How it was raining, raining much,
And how the drops of water soaked the ground.

Then, being ready, I started my trip.
The leaves of the trees formed a carpet,
And thus in quietness, lightly I stepped,
With concern in my soul.

Concerned about the conditions of the weather,
I stepped in the car and I wanted to start the engine,
But within myself I heard a voice telling me: "Do not be afraid,"
And thus I prayed to receive protection.

In this way I traveled to my workplace,
Hoping that the light of the day would soon appear,
And thus seeing how small we are in the face
Of all kinds of adverse situations.

The driving was difficult
And the visibility was low,
And I, under the influence of that beautiful voice,
Tried to temper my fear and to take it slow.

After almost an hour of driving,
I got to school while it was still dark;
Although it was a quarter past seven and in the morning,
The night covered everything like a fog.

Then I thanked God for His intent
To protect me from any accident
And because He helped me to arrive well at my destination,
Putting in me His inspiration.

The rain and the need to be a traveler
Made me to concentrate on You;
It made my need for You larger;
It made me look to You for help in all I had to do.

I thank You for Your faithfulness
And for the joy that is in You,
Because even in my weakness,
You receive me when I come to You.

The rain is good for the earth
And You send it to us by Your word
That the plants may grow,
Offering us beauty and food.

So it is also with Your Holy Spirit,
Who You give to us
When we receive You in thought and in deed,
Showing us how much You love us.

Your blessings over us overflow
And Your grace over us You bestow
In drops like those of the rain,
And always our lives You sustain.

October 30, 2009

THE SUN

When after the rain I see the beautiful rainbow,
I remember the covenant that You made,
Which will always remain and never fade,
A fact of the great past.

Then when the clouds go away and the sun appears,
I see the clear sky in its splendor;
And I rejoice, I feel the sun's heat,
And energy and life from it I receive.

All nature revives
And through Your care is encouraged;
It listens to Your voice
With great attention and desire.

You are the Bright Star, the Great Sun
Through Whose power our spirits are sustained;
You give us life and You maintain it,
And on our journey You help us to continue to run.

You are the brightest Sun,
Who gives us health with Your rays,
Carrying us through the phases of life
And making us victors that we may give You praise.

December 30, 2009

HAVE COURAGE

Have courage to face yourself,
To evaluate yourself, and to see how much good
Was imparted to you on your way,
Being carried in the holy arms.

Have courage to be what you were created to be,
And thus dare to come
To the cross of Golgotha,
Where you become confident and free.

Have courage to stay strong
For the eternal truth –
With boldness to proclaim it
And with all your life to live it.

Have courage to humble yourself
In the midst of a boastful world;
Have courage to repent and be bold
When there is only pride and hatred around you.

Have courage to be different
And to take the narrow path,
Knowing that you are loved by Jesus –
He who protects you from Satan's attack.

Have courage to be the support of the disadvantaged
And have courage to show love,
Knowing that you were called to this:
To give help and to receive it.

Have courage to recognize that you are limited
And that you are in need of help,
While also you are called to be useful
To a burdened soul.

Have courage to confront yourself
And to let yourself be transformed,
For thus to your troubled soul
Peace will return.

November 2, 2009

COME

Come from the path that you are on,
Come with your life's stories,
Come onto the good path,
To be together with the saints.

Come, while you still hear His call,
And do not let your heart harden;
Come that you may be refreshed
And that the Lord may meet you.

Come that you may be transformed
And in your soul and mind, changed;
Come to Jesus that you may receive forgiveness
And that in your soul you may carry a song in stillness.

Come to springs of living water –
Where you will find joy,
Where your past will be forgotten,
And where you will receive forgiveness.

Come to Jesus, Who died up on the cross
And Who subjected Himself to the heavenly Father,
That taking your sin and mine
He could save us from the most heavy yoke.

Come, therefore, and believe;
Do not be lost, but live.
For the time is advanced;
And the opportunity soon will have passed.

November 9, 2009

You Have Told Us

Traveling through life, going through different trials,
And walking upon difficult paths,
You have told me to have boldness and courage
In the voyage of life.

You have told me not to be afraid,
For in You everything is possible;
The impossible can become reality.

You have told us to come to You with confidence,
With prudence and with reverence,
For You have adopted us to be Yours,
Snatching us from this world of evil.

You bring to our remembrance
The fact that when we come to You,
We enter into Your presence
Through the sacrifice from the cross.

Jesus is the door through Whom I must pass,
And through Him I should attentively carry on
That I may arrive to the Father in heaven
And gaze upon His glory.

In the hour of pain and suffering
You have told us not to get discouraged,
But to give You our burdens
Through the power of faith.

You have told us not to be careless
And not to be overcome by fear,
But in quietness and thoughtfulness
To allow Your voice to speak to us and make our minds clear.

Let us have courage to live for You
When the world presses us and wants to prevail;
Let us have courage to proclaim Your name
And to look to You when all else around us fails.

November 12, 2009

I Come Before You

I come before You
To become new,
To know Your love
Which comes from above.

I give You my heart,
For that is my part;
It is all that I can bring,
And is the most important thing.

I give You my life
And my soul's strife,
And I embrace Your cross
With its gain and loss.

November 21, 2009

EARLY IN THE MORNING

Early in the morning,
When all is calm and quiet
The sun of Your love is shining.

Nature is still;
There is no wind, no sound,
Nothing loud.

It is an autumn day
And the sky is gray;
The trees are beautifully colored.

The leaves have fallen to the ground,
They are a part of Your creation
And our souls are bound
To Him Who brings us His salvation.

December 4, 2009

I am Just a Pilgrim

I am just a pilgrim in this world of sin,
And I come to You just as I am
So that You may cleanse and make me free;
I come to You, Divine Lamb.

I am just a pilgrim in this world of temptation,
And I need Your redemption;
I am called not to live a life of comfort
But rather to respond to You.

I am just a pilgrim in this world of confusion –
A world of ideas based on illusion,
A world with much grief and pain,
Where there are many who suffer while others gain.

I am just a pilgrim in this world of evil,
Full of problems and trials;
I am just passing by,
Confronted by both the truth and the lies.

I am just a pilgrim, living here for a short time,
Where there is sometimes joy sublime,
However I am reminded,
That with You I am united.

I am reminded that the joy may depart
And the two of us can grow apart.
How sad and painful that would be,
When the bond of love is broken.

November 8, 2009

I Have Found a Friend

In You I have found a friend for life
Who takes away my strife;
A friend Who loves me more than any other,
A friend Who is closer than a brother.

A friend Who died on the cross
And Who for me took great loss,
Of the heavenly glory divine,
In such a way that His love will be mine.

I have found a friend Whose body bled,
Showing me His love that led
My mind and soul to come to Him,
I have found a friend Whose body was torn

And thus hope was born;
A friend to Whom all power is given
To take us to heaven.

I have found a friend Who has brought me peace,
Who took me from the mire
And saved me from eternal fire.

I have found a friend Who walks with me
And wants to be by my side
That He may show me His care
And keep me from Satan's snare.

I have found a friend Who will reward
Anyone who follows His Word;
A friend Who for me stands
Because my condition He understands.

I have found a Friend who takes away
My burden, with all its weight,
And frees me from the power of sin,
Welcoming me in.

December 16, 2009

A Song

It is late in the night,
There is little light,
And I listen to a beautiful song.

It is quiet and only the music is heard.
It is close to Christmas,
And we remember that a Child was born to us
Just as the prophets foretold.

In my heart there is a song;
It takes me along,
It leads me to high peaks,
And great joy to me it brings.

There is a song of victory
And there is also a song of pain,
Yet in it there is much gain.

The song within me touches my heart;
It is a song that is aimed
Both towards God and towards mankind
And that transforms my mind –

A song that comes from eternity
And makes my heart with joy to leap,
A song that brings hope and health
And is by You so blessed.

December 16, 2009

BECAUSE OF YOU

Because of You, I wake up in the morning;
Because of You, I keep on going;
Because of You, I look around
And I see Your love abound.

Because of You, I keep on living;
Because of You, I keep on striving;
Because of You, I keep on hoping;
Because of You, I keep on helping;

Because of You, I look up
As through life I walk;
Because of You, I can dare
To show others that I care.

You have given me courage to stand
When all around me fails
And when evil prevails.

Because of You, I can look ahead
Despite all that is bad;
I can look ahead with confidence
And learn what faith is.

December 19, 2009

Jesus Christ the King

Good news to the world we bring:
That Jesus Christ is King –
King of kings and Lord of lords,
Prince of peace, ruler of all.

He came to show us how to live
And He wants to lead our lives
And to show us our need to repent,
So that we can be content.

Before He came, there was darkness,
Affliction from sin,
And much restlessness.

Then, the people who walked in darkness
Saw a great light;
The glory of God
Was seen in Jesus Christ's brightness.

He came as a Child,
Tender and mild;
As a Son, to us He was given,
And through Him we are forgiven.

The government will be on His shoulders
And His name is: "Wonderful, Counselor,
Mighty God, Everlasting Father,
Prince of Peace, King of kings;" He is our souls' lover.

The increase of His government
And peace will have no end.
His leadership is permanent
And so we should submit to Him, and not just pretend –

For He is a God of power,
A God of might, The Father of eternity,
A strong and protective Tower.

December 20, 2009

Truth and Falsehood

Truth is pure reality,
Whether good or bad;
Truth is spoken directly
Whether it is joyful or sad.

Truth is clear and sincere,
And it brings forth healing;
It is a precious treasure,
Strong and liberating.

Truth is gentle while powerful,
Though it can be a sword with two edges.
Yet it makes us grateful
In that it can build bridges.

Falsehood, though, is a distortion
Of what is good and noble;
It is a deterioration.

There is an evil power in falsehood
That is able to bring great strife
To a person's life.

Falsehood is cold and cruel;
It is an enticing fuel
Of further ills in a soul that is not redeemed
And has not received the salvation of the Lord.

Falsehood cannot be proven by the evidence;
It cannot stand and be believed;
It is only a pretense
And is never valid.

Falsehood is changeable,
Truth is stable;
Falsehood dies out in confusion,
But truth is not built on illusion.

In the end falsehood hurts and bites;
It leaves us scarred
And locked in a prison
Where there is no light.

Truth brings light
That gives us energy in our fight
And opens for us the gates of love,
By which we can find peace and hope from above.

Truth is clean and strong;
It disperses all wrong.
Truth does not behave furiously
But is calm and gives generously.

Truth does not use politeness
As a concealment for bitterness;
It is honest and it confronts.

Falsehood, though, is disguised
In compassion and interest,
But within us it brings great distress.

Politeness with truth is good –
It keeps us from being rude;
But politeness with falsehood
Cannot take the truth;

With truth, it brings freedom
And transports us to God's Kingdom;
But with falsehood, it brings anger
And selfishness that is shown to us later.

December 24, 2009

Blessed Are...

Psalm 119:1-11

Blessed are the undefiled
Who walk in Your way;
Blessed are those who seek You
With all their heart.

They do no iniquity,
For they walk in Your way;
You have commanded them to preserve their purity
And their lives before You to lay.

Oh, that my ways by You might be directed
That I may keep Your statues;
For then I will not be ashamed
When I will look to Your truths.

I will praise You with a pure heart
When I learn Your righteous judgments;
Help me to keep Your commandments
So that from You I will not depart.

In Your Word You say
That only in You can we keep our way clean –
By taking heed of Your Word
And following You, Lord.

Your Word I want to hide within my heart
So that of Your life I may take part
And that I may not sin against You,
For You can make me new.

At Your divine call
I bring before You my all
So that I may find salvation
And receive Your redemption.

March 7, 2010

In the Race of Life

In the race of life
You met me on my way,
And You taught me how to obey.

You met me in my distress
When I was in need
Of Your guidance and help.

You met me in my struggles
When within me there raged a battle.
When I was in despair,
I came to You in prayer.

The battle within me existed because I knew
About You and Your care,
But at the time was not among the few
Who wanted to bear Your name.

You met me in my wandering –
While I was pondering
Your will in my life,
While I was in strife.

When You met me,
You came to my rescue
And helped me to see.

You made me understand
That only in You can I stand,
That You are God the Father,
And that Jesus, Your Son, is our brother.

He is the first of all creation;
Through Him all that exists was made.
I know that Your Word will not fade,
For it comes from You with a definite purpose.

Your Word works through Your Holy Spirit,
And His power has no limit
In making us change and transform,
Giving to our lives a new form:

A form that is good and godly;
A form that reflects Your love and care
And that bears Your image,
Speaking of You powerfully.

Thus my direction is changed
And my life to You is pledged,
That I may live with a purpose in mind
And that towards others I may always be kind.

My search reaches an end
When I think of You and the promised land,
When I think of You and Your salvation
As I desire to put on Your perfection.

March 10, 2010

OPEN MY EYES

Open my eyes that I may see
Your hand at work in my life;
Help me, revive me,
And put an end to my strife.

Open my eyes that I may see my sin,
And help me to run to Your side.
For there I desire to abide;
On You I wish to lean.

I want to see the cross,
To understand the cost
Which You paid for me
At Calvary.

Open my eyes to see the fountain of forgiveness;
Open my eyes to understand Your meekness
That I may live according to Your precepts,
Keeping Your commandments

Open my heart to know
Not to rely upon anyone or anything,
But upon You alone
And to You only to cling.

Open my soul to Your love
Which sent You down to us –
Love that covered all my past
And brought healing from above.

Open my ears that I may hear
The powerful call
That You gave to us
To come near.

Open my mind, soul, and spirit
To receive Your healing;
Thus fill my cup up to its limit
As my life to You I bring.

March 21, 2010

His Arms are Still Open

His arms are still open
For everyone to come.
They are an expression of His love,
Though seen only by some.

He is still calling
For sinners to return to Him
While time still exists,
Even if their faith is dim.

The cross is the place
Where our burdens from us are taken
And where our sins are forgiven.

At the cross, salvation is offered,
For the price was paid in full,
And our lives to Him we surrender
So that they may become meaningful.

Jesus, on the cross You submitted to separation
From Your heavenly Father
So that You could bring us redemption
And become our brother.

You died in our place,
Taking the Father's judgment
So that we would not be condemned,
But some day see Your face.

Then, in the grave, the place where death lays,
You remained for three days;
But its grip could not hold You down –
You resurrected and walked right out.

His arms are still open wide
To receive all of us;
He desires to give us His might
And to be in our lives.

The power of the resurrection is today present
For all those who have witnessed the moment
Of Your intervention in their lives,
For all those who want to know Your love.

For there was a selection
Made from the foundation of the world
Of those chosen to become a royal generation,
Those who before Him could be bold.

You will know if you are selected
If to His call you respond –
If with your life you are not content
But rather you desire to break sin's bond.

March 30, 2010

WHEN THE SKY IS DARK

When the sky is dark and the clouds gather,
When the wind picks up and howls,
Then we know that a great storm follows
And nature's forces are coming together.

The storm hits and it destroys;
It takes with it all that lies in its way;
It seems not to obey
God's holy laws.

But after a while, it stops, all is calm,
And the sun comes out in all its brightness;
For I know that You hold me in Your palm
Because I am the branch and You are the vine.

Thus I again see Your power
Which You manifest in nature,
And I trust in You as my strong tower
And my wonderful treasure.

I see Your greatness again
As I bring to you my fear and pain;
For You love me so,
And I know that You watch over me here below.

April 9, 2010

WHEN SIN ABOUNDS

When I look around,
I see that all kinds of sins abound,
But I know that You are strong
And have the power to overcome all wrong.

You have offered to us salvation
And freedom from condemnation;
You ask us to tell this to the world,
To live for You and to be bold.

You have told us to be salt and light;
To live in Your might;
To have love, understanding, patience,
And a clean conscience;

To love You the most,
Despite any cost;
For You have loved us first
And have quenched our souls' thirst.

There is always room for another
To join with those who are in Your presence –
To bow down before You with reverence
And to allow Your love to penetrate to the core.

In Jesus, there is power that heals –
Power that fills one's soul
With strength, joy, and courage
And that helps him his life to manage.

In Him there is pleasure
That this world does not know:
There is a precious treasure
Of living waters that flow.

He calls us to buy this from Him without money
That we may revive our souls and minds;
That we may taste His love, which is sweeter than honey,
And learn from Him to be kind.

He asks us to love mercy and justice
And to put these into practice;
To receive Him as our Savior and Lord
And to stand in the power of His Word.

So, come just as you are;
Come from nearby or from afar;
For He wants to touch your life
And to show you so much.

He will give You a new mind and heart,
A purpose to live for,
Love, hope, endurance, and more;
He will set You apart.

When sin abounds,
His love is greater yet;
Our response to this love is what counts –
Our response to Him whose body bled.

Jesus loves sinners
And yet He judges the sin
That separates us from Him.
So, come, come, come to Him.

April 13, 2010

WALKING THROUGH LIFE

Walking through life,
I many times feel Your presence
And I know that You are by my side,
Wanting to accompany me in my every experience.

Trials of all kinds come
To test my commitment to You –
Pain they bring;
And tears, too –

Trials coming from the speech and actions
Of those most dear,
Hurting our relationship
Through many negative reactions.

Just when I thought we were close,
I have to witness the loss
Of the depth of our relationship
That had once underpinned our friendship:

A separation from one so lovely,
A separation from one so beautiful and smart
Due to our positions and our stands
On issues that can be hard to understand;

A deviation from what is good,
A separation that creates a mood
Of pain and regrets
As it wounds our hearts in so many respects.

But in these situations, Your name I call,
Because in it is great power
To heal, to bring Your salvation to all,
And to make us Your followers.

We need Your love and mercy,
Your strength in our weakness,
Your humility and Your meekness;
May these be our legacy.

We need a good heart and strong motivation,
Wisdom and determination
To be able to move on in life
Under the guidance of Your light.

Lord Jesus, come, restore my soul,
And help me to love my dear one as You love us;
Come and restore our trust
And let this be our main goal.

Teach us how to act, when we are under pressure,
According to the nature
Of the principles that You have taught
And the salvation that You have brought.

Give us sensibility,
Sensitivity, and the ability
To understand each other's heart,
So that we will not grow apart.

Help us to understand the art of communication,
To know the ways by which it develops,
To understand the power it holds
And also its limitations.

Help us to continue to relate to each other,
To love and protect one another,
To be of help and blessing;
Help us with our hearts' cleansing.

While we run this race,
Give us Your grace
That we may know how to share
And when is our time for prayer

A time of searching,
A time of healing,
A time of purging,
A time of refreshing;

A time of new beginnings
And a time of reconnecting.

May 3, 2010

Index

CPSIA information can be obtained
at www.ICGtesting.com
Printed in the USA
JSHW021321091122
32867JS00001B/68